I0129984

SOCIAL SECURITY PRINCIPLES

International Labour Office - Geneva

Copyright © International Labour Organization 1998

Publications of the International Labour Office enjoy copyright under Protocol 2 of the Universal Copyright Convention. Nevertheless, short excerpts from them may be reproduced without authorization, on condition that the source is indicated. For rights of reproduction or translation, application should be made to the Publications Bureau (Rights and Permissions), International Labour Office, CH-1211 Geneva 22, Switzerland. The International Labour Office welcomes such applications.

Libraries, institutions and other users registered in the United Kingdom with the Copyright Licensing Agency, 90 Tottenham Court Road, London W1P 9HE (Fax: + 44 171 436 3986), in the United States with the Copyright Clearance Center, 222 Rosewood Drive, Danvers, MA 01923 (Fax: + 1 508 750 4470) or in other countries with associated Reproduction Rights Organizations, may make photocopies in accordance with the licences issued to them for this purpose.

PREFACE

This manual is one of a series produced by the Social Security Department of the International Labour Office (ILO) Geneva, and was prepared in conjunction with the International Training Centre of the ILO, Turin.

Other manuals in the series :

- Administration of social security
- Social security financing
- Pension schemes
- Social health insurance
- A Trainers' Guide

The manuals have been produced primarily for use in countries where social security systems are not yet operational, are undergoing change or need to be improved. In particular, the manuals will be useful in developing countries, countries in transition, and countries undergoing structural change, as they begin the process of setting up new systems of social protection or of improving existing systems.

It should be noted, however, that the information contained in the manuals refers almost entirely to the formal sector and not to the wide range of systems which apply to groups outside the traditional social security system.

It will be apparent that, in a manual of this size, it is possible to provide only a broad overview of the topic. For the reader needing more extensive or detailed information about social security principles there may well be a need for additional reading. A range of publications deal with the topic in more depth and some of these are included in the further reading list at the end of this manual.

Thanks are due to all those people - too numerous to mention individually - who have helped in the preparation of this manual. In particular it should be noted that it draws heavily on two earlier ILO productions: "Social security - A workers' education guide" and "Introduction to social security".

Should any reader wish to provide comments or feedback on the contents of this or any other manual in the series, please write to:

The International Labour Office
SEC/SOC, 9th. Floor
4 route des Morillons
CH-1211 GENEVA 22
Switzerland
Fax (22)799.7962

TABLE OF CONTENTS

INTRODUCTION

From earliest times human beings have sought to protect themselves and their dependants and to provide a better and safer environment in which to live. In short, people need security.

For many generations, people have been trying to find systems, based on the principle of mutual solidarity, for purposes of coping with different forms of hardship. In the modern world, tackling the issue of social protection is a major yardstick for gauging a country's political determination to ensure maximum mobilization of human resources in the national economic effort.

Many, though not all, industrialized countries have set up effective national social security systems which are often complemented by private insurance schemes and which, together, guarantee virtually full coverage for all beneficiaries.

The same seldom applies, however, to developing countries, where the family structure continues to bear the strain and cost of health and family welfare.

This manual focuses on the concept and practice of *social security*, one of the main pillars on which overall security rests. While the term *social security* may mean different things to different people, there is one common thread, that of the natural desire of communities for greater protection protection from life's problems, from uncertainty, from disease and deprivation.

Over the last two centuries, men and women have become increasingly reliant, for the standard and quality of their life, on cash wages and on the goods and services provided by others. In the absence of wages or income they have often been unable to cushion themselves and their families from the uncertainties of life.

Over a period of time, like-minded individuals have banded together for mutual self-protection to try to ease their problems when income, on which they have come to rely, is reduced or ceases. This has not always been easy and in many countries, even today, there are communities that still have little or no protection.

In countries which are more fortunate, the infrastructure needed to meet the ordinary requirements of citizens - in such areas as education, housing, health care, income replacement and employment - is very well developed. Even in those countries, however, there are problems which still have to be overcome and new ones continue to emerge as a result of social and economic changes and developments.

This manual is aimed at those who wish to know more about social security; what it is, what it provides, what difficulties there are in furnishing adequate protection, and so on. It can do no more than provide a broad overview and the most it can achieve is to present, from the standpoint of the International Labour Organization (ILO), what needs to be understood about the main aspects of social security programmes.

It is necessary, at the outset, to attempt to provide a definition of social security, to give a brief outline of its historical development, and to mention some of the different types of schemes which are currently in operation. Further sections of the Manual look at who is protected by social security and make broad reference to some of the social security benefits - of which there are nine main types - and the qualifying conditions.

Only a brief reference will be made to the financing of social security schemes and the effect of social security on the economies of countries because there is a separate manual in this series which examines financing in much greater detail.

Since an efficient administration is vital for the successful running of schemes, the manual also makes reference to some aspects of administration - though, again, only very briefly as the series also includes a manual dealing with social security administration.

A short section is included in this Manual on the special arrangements which may be made for migrant workers and the final module presents a summary of the ILO's role in the development of social security.

SOCIAL SECURITY PRINCIPLES

MODULE 1:
WHAT IS SOCIAL SECURITY?

International Labour Office - Geneva

MODULE CONTENTS

MODULE 1

WHAT IS SOCIAL SECURITY ?

UNIT 1: Introduction to social security

A. History and definitions

What is social security all about?

Social security covers a wide spectrum and affects the daily life of vast numbers of people throughout the world. Limits therefore need to be set when attempting to give a historical background and provide definitions. First, the term "daily life" is not strictly accurate because social security often starts *before* birth - with the provision of pre-birth care and maternity benefits - and continues *after* death, with the payment of some form of death benefit.

Reference was made in the Introduction to the need and search for greater individual and group security which has always been present as people tried to protect themselves and their families from hunger, pestilence and other dangers which threatened or surrounded them. Providing the necessities to sustain life - shelter, food and clothing - has been a continual battle and this still remains a constant and ongoing problem for a large proportion of the world's population.

As the centuries unfolded, communities organized themselves into groups of various types. Initially, this was in order to protect themselves from the physical dangers which surrounded them and, later, to attempt to lessen some of the harsher aspects of life. In the course of time, people with similar problems and concerns joined together for mutual protection. Trade and artisan guilds were formed with the aim of helping members when hardship struck, and many religious institutions helped to alleviate some of the misery of those who were unable to cope with life's problems.

During the nineteenth century, the individual, rural, way of life - with many people living off the land, often in poor circumstances - gave way to industrialization, particularly in large parts of Europe. This change posed new social and economic problems and was accentuated by the drift away from rural to urban areas, in which commercial and industrial development was taking place and where wage employment was to be found.

Workers in industry became reliant on the regular payment of wages for food, shelter and clothing, and in the absence of such wages they lacked the traditional "social shield" which helped to protect them and their families from the worst excesses of deprivation. That "social shield" had previously consisted of the clan and tribal systems, and the extended family, in which the able-bodied helped to look after children, the frail, the elderly and the weak. It was no longer available, however, in the urban situation.

Piecemeal attempts were made to lessen the distress of those whose wages stopped because of sickness, unemployment, work injury or old age. Savings schemes were organized by governments or mutual aid societies. Private insurance developed and provided life cover and funeral benefits. States began to introduce legislation which required employers to provide some maintenance for their sick or injured workers but these arrangements were not sufficient in themselves. The philosophy of the day was that workers could and should make their own arrangements to counteract life's risks yet they were so absorbed in the day-to-day struggle for survival that it was unrealistic to expect them to anticipate or plan for possible or distant eventualities.

Against this background, at first slowly but with a quickening pace once labour became more organized, more vocal and more powerful, social protection programmes began to take shape in industrialized countries. These early programmes were often compulsory, applying initially to certain categories of worker but progressively being extended to cover large sections of the population. Various benefits were introduced which sought to replace - at least in part - lost wages and incomes. With the passage of time, these benefits were extended and eventually the term "social security" was used to collectively describe them.

A widely accepted definition of "social security" is:
" .... the protection which society provides for its members - through a series of public measures - against the economic and social distress that otherwise would be caused by the stoppage, or substantial reduction, of earnings resulting from sickness, maternity, employment injury, unemployment, invalidity, old age and death; the provision of medical care; and the provision of subsidies for families with children."

It is interesting to note that the term "social security" was first used officially in United States legislation of 1935 - the Social Security Act, 1935 - and it also appeared in an Act passed in New Zealand in 1938. Following the second world war, an increasing number of countries introduced and developed social welfare programmes and the ILO subsequently used the term "social security" extensively in several ILO Conventions and Recommendations*, which sought to establish the standards which countries should follow in the years following 1952. Increasingly, the term "social security" became more and more widely used and today is understood the world over.

Fig. 1:
"Social Security ...
is understood the world
over ..."

It should be remembered that social security is composed of several different elements: social insurance; social assistance; benefits financed by the general revenues of a country; family benefits; and provident funds. These must also be linked to additional provisions which are made by employers, notably workers' compensation schemes (in respect of accidents or diseases of occupational origin) and other complementary programmes which have developed around social security.

---

*Conventions and Recommendations are dealt with in detail in Module 6, Unit 1 of this Manual

B. Social insurance and social assistance

Social insurance

Social insurance was first established in Germany, more than a century ago, when local governments set up sickness funds to which workmen were required to pay compulsory contributions. When an illness occurred, benefits were then paid to the insured workman. These first sickness insurance schemes were followed by similar schemes which covered other contingencies - employment injury, invalidity and old age. All of the social partners - workers, employers and the State - had a say in the running of the schemes and it should be noted that worker solidarity played a prominent role in the conception, establishment and running of the schemes.

The concept of insurance is based on the principle of the pooling of risks. This requires that everyone who is involved in and covered by the scheme makes a contribution to a common fund. When and if a contributor meets the prescribed conditions for benefit - for example, suffers an illness and has paid sufficient contributions over a specific period - his or her needs (or at least part of them) are met from the insurance fund.

Social insurance schemes may differ, one from another, but the principal elements of all schemes are:

- they are financed by contributions, normally shared between workers and employers, often with some State participation;

- they require compulsory participation;

- contributions are paid into special funds, from which benefits are paid;

- surplus funds are invested to earn additional income;

- benefits are guaranteed, on the basis of the contribution record, *without* means testing (i.e. they do not take income or wealth into account);

- contributions and benefits are often proportionate to earnings;

- employment injury schemes are usually wholly financed by employers.

Social assistance

Some countries began - or have subsequently redesigned - their social security programmes on what is referred to as "social assistance" lines. In such schemes, taxes - either local or national - are used to finance various programmes providing benefits which are paid, as a right, when the prescribed conditions of need are met. Generally speaking, "means" (usually including income and capital) are taken into account when arriving at the assessment of the benefit to be paid.

Many countries which rely primarily on social insurance programmes also operate social assistance schemes for those persons who - for one reason or another - fall outside the scope of the main programme, or whose social insurance benefits are insufficient to meet their needs. Since social assistance and social welfare are closely related, some discretion is often exercised when deciding the amount or type of payment to be made.

Australia, New Zealand and some Scandinavian countries are examples of countries which have opted for a social assistance approach to social security.

UNIT 2: Other routes to social security

A. Benefits from general revenue

In yet other countries standard benefits for all residents, or for persons who have been in employment for a requisite length of time, may be awarded and paid *irrespective* of means. Such benefits often include pensions for the elderly, for those who are widowed or orphaned, and for invalids; which are all financed from the general revenues of the State. Medical care is also provided in some countries without the need for contributions or a means test, again with the cost being met, wholly or partially, from public funds.

B. Family benefits

There are many countries which provide some form of social security payment in recognition of the special needs and additional expenditure associated with raising a family. In some countries, arrangements are made through the taxation structure to take account of family responsibilities. There are others, however, which provide special benefits to those who are raising a child/children, either by way of a pension or by supplementing wages.

C. Provident funds

Provident funds and societies concerned with thrift and savings have existed for generations. In the absence of other forms of social protection, they responded to the special needs of groups of like-minded individuals who wished to save in order to meet future expenditure. Many States, particularly those whose economies were still in the process of development, subsequently adapted the approach and introduced national schemes which were generally known as "national provident fund schemes". These had the advantage of being an easily understood form of national and compulsory savings and, in such schemes, the accumulated contributions (savings) are paid out to members - together with added interest from the return on investment - when particular contingencies occur (commonly old age, invalidity or death).

Meanwhile, the funds remaining can be used for social and economic development projects.

In provident fund schemes, individual contributions are deducted from workers' wages, when employed, and these are usually matched by a similar (or sometimes greater) contribution from employers; the combined contribution is placed into an account in the name of the worker which is maintained by the provident fund institution.

Some would say that a national provident fund scheme is not a "true social security scheme" in the conventional sense for: there is no pooling of risks among the covered workers; rarely are there periodical payments in lieu of wages as most provident fund schemes pay benefits by lump sum payments. Unfortunately also, in inflationary situations, the accumulating contributions can lose much of their purchasing power so that the benefit which is ultimately paid often has little relationship to the cost of living.

D. Employers' provision

Employers' liability schemes exist in many countries. These are mainly concerned with the risk of employment injury (accidents at work and occupational diseases) and they place an onus on the employer to provide compensation and medical care in respect of employment injury - either directly or under an approved insurance policy. Most schemes of this type are known as *workers' compensation schemes*.

Labour laws, which have been introduced in many countries, have also required employers to provide compulsory benefits of a social security type. This has resulted in the introduction, by many countries, of payments during sickness and maternity leave. Indemnities have also been provided when a worker is dismissed or is made redundant. The obligation to provide medical care is also found in some legislations, and more and more employers have been encouraged by States - through tax and other incentives or concessions - to create occupational pension plans, either to replace or to supplement the existing social security provisions. While the latter are usually non-statutory - (that is, they are not included in an Act of Parliament) - such arrangements are increasing, both in number and scope, and are a fruitful area for collective bargaining and industrial agreements.

E. Social services

Depending on the resources which are available to it - and as a part of its overall social protection - the State often provides *social services* to its citizens. In the absence of social service provision, or perhaps because the available services are inadequate, voluntary and other organisations frequently attempt to fill some of the gaps in provision.

Social services usually include:

- preventive action in health care (i.e. prevention of diseases such as cholera or typhoid) by educating people about proper sanitation, accident avoidance; by undertaking inoculation programmes, etc.;

- rehabilitation of the injured and disabled;

- the provision of special facilities for the disabled and the elderly;

- the provision of child care and welfare;

- the provision of advice and assistance with family planning.

Sometimes these services are fully integrated with other elements of social security; in this respect, much will depend on the historical development of a country's social security system as a whole.

F. The spread of social security

The aftermath of the Second World War saw a rapid increase in the number of countries which introduced - or extended their existing - social security measures. At the same time, many countries had achieved - or were in the process of achieving - independence and, as part of their reconstruction efforts, wished to broaden social protection for their citizens. It was not possible to rely exclusively on collective or individual efforts of workers or employers to organize comprehensive coverage on a national basis and the State had to take the lead. It is interesting to note the progression, over the years, of the number of state-sponsored social security programmes and Table 1 gives an indication of their extent.

Table 1: The growth in social security programmes

Type of programme	1940	1949	1958	1967	1977	1989	1995
All	57	58	80	120	129	145	165
Old-age/invalidity survivors	33	44	58	92	114	135	158
Sickness/ maternity	24	36	59	65	72	84	105
Employment injury	57	57	77	117	129	136	159
Unemployment	21	22	26	34	38	40	63
Family benefits	7	27	38	62	65	63	81

Source: United States Department of Health and Human Services., *Social security programmes throughout the world, 1995*, Research report No. 62 (Washington, DC, 1995).

It will be noted that employment injury benefit coverage is a feature of more than 95% of the countries and almost an equal number have also made provision for old-age, invalids and survivors. "Short-term" benefits, in respect of sickness and maternity - and so called because they are generally expected to be only of short duration - are provided in fewer countries, about 63%. Family allowances were being paid in rather less than 50% of the countries. Although benefits in respect of unemployment are available in most industrialized countries - even if only for a limited duration - it will be seen that this represents only about 38% of the total.

SOCIAL SECURITY PRINCIPLES

MODULE 2:
WHO IS PROTECTED
BY SOCIAL SECURITY?

International Labour Office - Geneva

MODULE CONTENTS

MODULE 2

WHO IS PROTECTED BY SOCIAL SECURITY ?

UNIT 1: Persons protected

A. Is total coverage possible?

It would be ideal if *every* member of a community could be protected by social security, whatever the individual's station in life; in other words if the coverage could be truly universal. Such protection would be an expression of the solidarity of the community as a whole; indeed this concept underlies the whole idea of social security. It would also be ideal if the protection could be uniform, across the community.

What is *ideal*, however, is not always *practicable*. Even in those countries which have the most advanced forms of social protection, it cannot be claimed that each and every individual has complete or adequate coverage. Conditions and lifestyles change and what was thought to be just and adequate 20 or 30 years ago may no longer be appropriate today. For reasons of history, culture, religion or tradition, some social security programmes are given greater emphasis than others. Political and economic conditions also have to be taken into account when making decisions about which schemes are suitable or appropriate.

Fig. 2:
"... what is ideal ... is not always practicable ..."

When formal social security programmes were first introduced, they tended to be based purely on social insurance principles. They were often very limited in their coverage, for example by including only certain types of workers - coalminers, railwaymen, workers in factories employing more than 20 persons, workers in certain towns or regions, etc.. Even today, many countries are unable to proceed as quickly as they would wish in putting into place even the most limited coverage of the population - let alone a universal scheme.

One reason for this is that it is rarely possible to cover every individual in the community from the outset of a scheme. Most countries therefore make a start by covering those sectors which are reasonably well organized and where the individual workers can be readily identified, for this eases the task of administration. As the country - and, in particular, the social security institution - gains experience in running the scheme, it can then be gradually extended to cover other sectors and thus to an ever increasing number of people.

Previous reference has been made to some of the ILO Conventions relating to social security. One of the most important is the Social Security (Minimum Standards) Convention, 1952 (No. 102). This Convention brought together, in one comprehensive document, the policies to which member States were prepared to subscribe at that time. As well as describing and defining a range of benefits which are at the heart of social security, it lays down minimum requirements as to: coverage of the population; the content and the level of benefits; contributors' and beneficiaries' rights; and how schemes should be administered.

The Convention lists nine distinct branches of social security (referred to briefly on page 8 and in more detail in Module 3) and, in so far as coverage of the population is concerned, the minimum level demanded by the Convention is relatively modest. In some of the branches, it is necessary to have coverage of no more than 50 per cent of the persons at risk, before being able to ratify the Convention. Even within the main standards set by the Convention, a country whose "economy and medical facilities are insufficiently developed" may avail itself of temporary exceptions when applying for ratification. The idea is to encourage countries to make a start on adopting the Convention, rather than to impose conditions that are too restrictive. Further references will be made to Convention 102 throughout the Manual.

B. *The effect of administrative procedures*

One of the many reasons for the uneven coverage of populations, briefly referred to earlier, is the administration factor. Where individuals and employers contribute to a social security scheme it is clearly necessary to keep details of employment, wages and, in particular, social security contributions so that, when benefit is claimed, the necessary information is available to enable the claim to be processed. In the case of "long-term" benefits (old-age pension, invalidity and survivors' benefits) contributions will be paid over many decades and must be properly recorded. Keeping accurate records over such long periods is a tremendous task even where the most up to date technology and data processing techniques are used. Although these can greatly ease the recording task, the administrative demands and challenges for a new social security institution are enormous.

One aspect of the administration which places a heavy demand on social security institutions is the registration of workers and employers. When a contributory scheme is first introduced, each individual member and employer covered by the scheme must be *individually* registered. Where a country already has a well-established system of civil registration, or uses national identity cards, these can perhaps be helpful to the social security registration process. The initial registration process must be completed quickly in order to provide each worker with a social security number as soon as possible after registration. It is important that workers are not registered more than once, for this will certainly cause subsequent problems for the correct allocation of future contributions to individual accounts.

The administrative demands which the registration process presents is a common reason for concentrating, first, on those members of a community who are most easily reached and identifiable, for whom formal employer records are most likely to exist and, therefore, who can be registered relatively easily and quickly. It is therefore common practice to include workers from the larger enterprises in a scheme's initial coverage - so as to immediately bring into the scheme a substantial proportion of the workforce. The hope is that, in due course, there will be a progressive extension of coverage to the remaining workers.

In several countries, however, where the early intention was to extend coverage in this way, it has not yet been possible to do so. Many workers in small enterprises, or in private domestic employment, or those working on a casual basis, therefore remain uncovered many years after the introduction of a scheme.

C. Concentration on the employed sector

There are, of course, many individuals in addition to employed persons who form part of society including, for example: persons who work on their own account - the self-employed; those who are not employed at all; and those who work in the home but receive no wages. Such groups and individuals are difficult to include in an insurance-based social security scheme.

From the point of view of an employed worker, one of the attractions which social insurance has to offer is its apparent value. Although workers pay a part of their wage as a contribution towards benefits, that contribution is almost always (at least) doubled by the employer; indeed the State may also add a supplement. Self-employed and non-employed persons, on the other hand, will have to meet the cost of the *full* contribution themselves and may find it difficult, if not impossible, to pay. Furthermore, where the country has a large proportion of self-employed persons among its citizens (such as small shopkeepers, agricultural small holders, taxi drivers, roadside artisans, etc.) there are many problems associated with identification, securing proper compliance with the social security legislation, and particularly with non-payment of contributions. Various methods have been tried in order to extend coverage to these "informal" sector workers, but with mixed success.

The fact is that most social insurance schemes concentrate on including those workers who normally rely on paid and formal employment for their livelihood, leaving other sections of the community to make their own arrangements. For those who suffer hardship, provision may be made through social assistance or universal schemes financed from general revenues.

There are a number of other areas where difficulties arise in applying the principles of universal and uniform coverage, even among employees themselves, and reference is made to some of these in the following unit.

UNIT 2: Causes of unequal coverage

A. *Higher paid employees*

Employees earn different levels of wages and salaries and in the early days of insurance-based social security schemes it was the practice (and still remains so in countries with certain forms of work-related accident legislation) to exclude higher-paid workers from social security coverage. This was usually on the grounds that higher paid workers were probably less at risk and, in any case, were considered to more easily be able to afford to cover themselves by personal insurance. When *flat-rate* contributory schemes were developed, which gave the same benefit rates to each worker, higher paid workers were *compulsorily* covered. However, they were at the same time at a disadvantage for they paid the same rate of contribution as the majority of workers (contribution levels being set at a rate which the *majority* of workers could afford to pay) but that rate was disproportionately low in relation to *their* salary or wage. When they subsequently became beneficiaries, the flat-rate benefit usually failed to meet their needs.

For this and other reasons, the "earnings-related" system of social security came into being. The benefits paid by an earnings related scheme are - as the title indicates - related to the member's lost or interrupted earnings; when employed, contributions are paid at a rate determined in accordance with the member's level of earnings. That being said, there is usually a maximum rate of benefit payable, which is prescribed under the legislation, and often a "ceiling" is also placed on the actual contribution to be paid; this means that contributions are paid *only* on earnings up to a specific level - not on earnings above that level.

B. *Occupational pension plans*

In many countries, some groups of workers were already covered by sectoral or employer-based pension protection at the time when general social security measures were being planned. These kinds of pension arrangements had often been established following pressure for such provisions by trade unions. Generally, however, this type of scheme only covered limited sections of the total labour force and frequently suffered from deficiencies, one of which was the lack of "portability". This meant that individual workers were unable to carry over their pension rights, which had been acquired with one employer, to another employer when they changed jobs.

The problem of how to coordinate existing occupational plans with new social security schemes has, for many countries, proved very difficult to resolve. On the one hand, the interests of solidarity require that all workers - from whatever group, section or background - should become members of a general social security scheme. On the other hand, however, many of the workers covered by such schemes do not take too kindly to the idea that they should surrender all or part of, what they regard as, this special and hard-fought-for arrangement. Additionally, some employers have used their occupational schemes to "encourage" their most prized workers to remain in their employment - because when workers leave employment which is accompanied by pension rights, those rights are often terminated too.

A number of solutions to this problem have been tried and these include: letting workers "opt out" of the general scheme, if they have adequate pension coverage; arranging for the social security scheme to take over the occupational pension funds and their assets and liabilities; allowing the occupational plan, in a full or revised form, to continue as an additional tier - or supplement - to social security provisions.

In industrialized countries, there has been a trend in recent years towards supplementary pension schemes. Encouragement has been given by many governments for the introduction of such schemes, which are additional to the general social security scheme and the benefits provided thereunder. This trend may well have resulted from the perceived overall inadequacy of social security pensions and from the financial pressures being exerted on scarce social security resources.

C. *Government and parastatal workers*

In most countries, government workers have, for many years, been covered by their own special and comprehensive protection measures established by legislation. These measures relate not only to terms of service and working conditions, but also to the provision of benefits when they have accidents at work, fall sick, become invalids or retire. The pensions and other benefits paid to public service workers are usually provided out of public funds, in the same way as are their wages or salaries. In one sense these pension plans can be seen simply as occupational pension plans operated by the government in its capacity as an employer. In another sense government workers, because of the nature of their employment, are in a rather special category since once they are "permanently" appointed they often continue in employment for the whole of their working life and only in very special circumstances are they likely to be dismissed. There are a number of good reasons for this approach - not least that it helps to create a public service which is not subject to political bias.

Yet, although this still holds true for most countries, there are some which are beginning to move away from the concept of "expect to be a public servant for life" and where, increasingly, service in the public sector may be only on a short-term contract basis, or where a period in the public service is just one part of a "mixed career" in both the public and private sector.

Nevertheless, when the policies for developing or expanding a national social security scheme are being considered, it is necessary to consider whether, in the interest of solidarity, civil servants should be incorporated into the scheme or excluded because of their special position, work and benefit conditions. This is all the more important in countries where the working population includes a large proportion who are employed in the government service. Similar considerations may also apply to parastatal workers for whom, in many countries, the legislation which governs their occupational benefits and pension is often based on that which applies to government workers.

D. Rural areas and agricultural workers

Social security was originally developed to meet the economic needs of urban, industrialized workers. Rural and agricultural workers clearly also have specific social and economic needs - in many cases, perhaps even more so than their urban counterparts - but it has proved difficult to extend conventional social security programmes to rural areas. Agricultural patterns vary greatly from country to country and from region to region. At one end of the spectrum are the large farms worked by wage labour and at the other are the subsistence smallholdings, tribal lands, sharecropping and seasonal labour systems. Such diverse arrangements make "standard" social security programmes difficult to develop and, in many countries, little or no social protection is provided for the rural sector.

The way ahead may be to develop new and innovative forms of social protection for agricultural workers and these might consist, for example, of crop and natural disaster insurance, better and guaranteed prices, guaranteed markets for produce, good health care services, etc..

Fig. 3:
"Social Security ... meets the needs of urban, industrialised workers ...

... may be a need to develop new ... innovative forms ... of social protection ... for agricultural workers"

E. *Voluntary contributors*

In an endeavour to extend coverage to as wide a selection of the population as possible, a number of countries make provision for people, who were previously compulsorily insured, to become voluntary contributors to the social insurance scheme, or - in the case of provident funds - to continue to be members of the fund.

In this way they can continue to build up their insurance or provident fund records and subsequently meet the eligibility requirements of the scheme. This provision is often also extended to the self-employed (in schemes which do not yet include the self-employed on a compulsory basis) and a number of schemes even permit the non-employed to contribute voluntarily. However, although this is a commendable idea it does raise some special difficulties.

The main problem, with any type of voluntary arrangement, is that they are not easy to administer effectively and to oversee. Firstly, this is because it is often difficult to collect the contributions once an individual has chosen to start paying voluntarily. Secondly, it is necessary to guard against the situation whereby the voluntary contributor pays contributions at an artificially high level simply in order to obtain benefits at a higher level than are appropriate. This phenomenon is usually referred to as "benefit-inspired contributions" and the problem is notoriously difficult to deal with and control. Thirdly, the arrangements must be closely monitored to ensure that advantage is not being taken of the scheme by people or groups who are "high risks" and who may adversely affect the prospects of other members of the scheme.

SOCIAL SECURITY PRINCIPLES

MODULE 3:
OUTLINE OF
SOCIAL SECURITY BENEFITS

International Labour Office - Geneva

MODULE CONTENTS

UNIT 1:   **An overview**

    A.   The general structure

    B.   The development of social insurance benefits

    C.   Distinctions between social insurance
       and other programmes

    D.   Qualifying conditions

    E.   Benefit levels and maintaining their value

UNIT 2:   **Benefits and their aims**

    A.   Medical care benefit

    B.   Sickness, maternity and funeral benefit

    C.   Employment injury benefit
       and workmen's compensation

    D.   Old-age benefit

    E.   Survivor's benefit

    F.   Invalidity benefit

    G.   Unemployment benefit

    H.   Family benefit

MODULE 3

OUTLINE OF
SOCIAL SECURITY BENEFITS

UNIT 1   An overview

A. *The general structure*

The Manual has, so far, briefly reviewed the development of social security and drawn attention to some of the difficulties in applying it, on a national basis, globally. Some of the attempts to overcome the problems involved in developing and extending social security have also been touched upon. This Module takes a look at social security from the viewpoint of the benefits which are provided by social security schemes.

The aim of social security is to provide assistance, financial or otherwise, in the event of loss or reduction of income. Originally, social insurance provided some measure of income replacement when earnings were interrupted or had ceased completely. However, it was only of partial use to receive financial help, for sickness, accident or invalidity, if adequate arrangements did not exist for the *medical care* of those suffering from poor health. In order to remedy this deficiency, many schemes began to include provision for health or medical care in their social protection programmes.

At one time it was hoped that social insurance provision would be adequate to meet the continuing needs of a scheme's members or that it would at least greatly reduce the need for social assistance measures. This has proved to be too optimistic for there are always those who have special requirements, or who fall outside the scope of social insurance (or other) schemes, and society cannot avoid its responsibilities for them. Programmes have therefore been established (or existing measures adapted) to take care of the particular needs of this section of the community.

In the most advanced social security programmes, social insurance forms just one part of a comprehensive range of social benefits. "Social transfers" are made which form a complex, interwoven system of redistribution of cash, goods and services to the needier sections of the community. Some ways in which these social transfers are accomplished are by way of tax allowances, subsidized housing and food, provision of transportation and free health care, as well as through means-tested benefits or allowances.

It cannot be claimed that the types of protection which have evolved in industrialized countries can easily be "adopted" by countries which are still in the course of development. The perception of people in industrialized communities, of their needs (and the priorities which they attach to them) is not necessarily the same as those of their next-door neighbours, let alone of people in other parts of the world. Each country must therefore develop its own programme, determining its own needs in the light of its available resources, and taking into account the aspirations of its people. For this reason, the ILO, when setting standards, has taken care to make those standards as flexible as possible in order to take account of a wide range of differing circumstances.

Thus, Convention No. 102 groups benefits in a way which has regard to their functions and only imposes the minimum of conditions, which *all* countries - industrialized and developing - can build upon as and when the time is appropriate.

The benefits referred to in the Convention are nine in all and are as follows:

- medical care
- sickness benefit
- maternity benefit
- unemployment benefit
- family benefit
- employment injury benefit
- invalidity benefit
- old-age benefit
- survivors' benefit.

It may have been noticed that, with the exception of unemployment benefit, all have some biological association - childbirth, rearing children, disease, injury, old age and death - and any or all of these may affect a worker's income.

B. The development of social insurance benefits

It has been seen that, even in countries with comprehensive schemes for benefits and coverage, there are still those who fall outside the schemes. Most countries are only able to introduce social security schemes in stages and even the most successful ones started relatively slowly, with the introduction of benefits which were non-controversial. Thus, benefits of the employment injury type tended to be introduced first and further extension was determined by what each individual country perceived as the next priority protection. Some countries, particularly those which were already experiencing the progressive breakdown of the extended family, considered that the problems associated with providing for the elderly was a priority. Others considered that medical care, sickness and maternity protection were of more immediate importance, while yet others concentrated on the provision of family benefits.

What is most important, however, is that a country's social protection programme should be considered as a whole, from the outset, and the pace of development should have full regard to the ability of the country, and its institutions, to organize and administer the programme effectively and efficiently.

While benefits provided through social insurance programmes were often introduced in response to pressure from organized labour, they were often also extended to self-employed persons, wherever it became possible to do so. However, it has already been seen that extending coverage and benefits to the self-employed is often difficult to achieve. Certain benefits, particularly unemployment and employment injury benefits, are extremely difficult to administer if extended to the self-employed and, for this reason, are rarely made available to them.

C. Distinctions between social insurance and other programmes

Because social insurance schemes often faced difficulties in extending coverage to particular groups (some of which have already been referred to - the self-employed, non-employed, agricultural workers, etc) social assistance or general revenue programmes were developed, either as replacements for social insurance programmes or as a supplement to them.

The basic difference between these programmes and social insurance is that:

- *social insurance* relies on membership of a scheme, *to* which contributions are paid, and *from* which benefits are provided to the member, or his/her family, when one of the stipulated contingencies occurs ;

- in *social assistance* or *general revenue programmes*, the right to benefit flows from membership of the community - and the community itself finds the necessary funds for the provision of benefit.

The distinction between the two types of programme is, however, tending to become somewhat blurred in a number of countries.

Where the funds to meet benefits come from the "entire community" - as is the case with social assistance and general revenue financed schemes - there is no need to keep the detailed contribution or employment records, over many years, which a social insurance scheme requires. The *sole* criterion for the right to benefit in social assistance/general revenue schemes is the satisfaction of a citizenship or a residence condition.

D. *Qualifying conditions*

The fact remains that for the majority of countries the goal of providing a fully comprehensive social protection programme is still a long way off. Social insurance remains a starting-point, however, even though in every scheme - including the most comprehensive ones - there are certain conditions which have to be met before a person can qualify for benefit, if for no other reason than to protect the funds and to prevent abuse.

The first condition must always be that the contingency, for which the benefit was designed, has indeed occurred. With some contingencies, for example childbirth, this is readily evident but others, like accidents at work, are less obvious and will therefore need to be proved. The person who claims an old-age pension will have to show that the required age has been reached; those who are sick will need to produce medical evidence, and so on.

Secondly, it will be necessary to show that the person concerned *is* covered by the scheme, i.e. that they are "contributing members". Thirdly, in order to protect the fund and its members, the claimant must have the necessary period of insurance or residence. Finally, the claimant must also be able to show that the various rules, stipulated in the legislation for the award of benefit to be made, are being adhered to.

In social assistance or general revenue financed schemes, there is *no* personal membership and insurance is *not* a requirement for the receipt of benefit. In most cases, the individual claimant's means are assessed and proof of residence is usually necessary, the required period of residence being greater for the longer-term benefits (e.g. old-age or invalidity) than for benefits of only short duration.

Very often the rules set limits as to the amount and duration of benefits and special conditions may apply to medical care benefits, such as the necessity for the claimant to follow the course of treatment prescribed by the medical authorities.

E. Benefit levels and maintaining their value

Benefit levels

Social security benefits are not "free" - they have to be paid for. The total sum paid out from a national social security scheme may be very considerable, indeed in many cases it will represent a large proportion of the national wealth. When planning for social protection, it is necessary to consider how much a country can afford when balancing the various social and economic considerations which must be taken into account. This is not an easy task and is often a controversial matter which generates fierce debate and requires compromise. ILO Conventions recognize that there must be a great deal of flexibility when putting forward standards for the levels of benefit. Generally there are two approaches to this.

The first approach is to base benefit levels on a proportion of the wages normally earned; benefits payable under this system are referred to as *earnings-related benefits*. The second is to base them on the cost of subsistence and these are referred to as *flat rate benefits*. Those who drafted Convention No. 102 went to a great deal of trouble in attempting to establish fair and reasonable rules, having regard to the varying economic situations in different countries. For example, there is a method of arriving at a "typical wage" for the country concerned and for measuring the adequacy of the benefit level by reference to that "typical wage". Where the scheme is intended to provide flat rate subsistence levels of benefit, the Convention indicates that reference is to be made to the wage of a typical, *unskilled*, male worker. In an earnings related scheme, however, the benefits should be related to the wages of a *skilled* manual worker.

In practical terms, there are limits to the types and levels of benefit provided but it is rare to find benefits, in respect of lost earnings, to be less than 25% of the wage of an *unskilled* worker and there are even countries where the replacement rate reaches 100 per cent of an individual's wage. Many countries, however, set maximum rates of benefit.

The reason for the differences between one country and another lies in the variations of economic, philosophical and cultural patterns, and in the approaches adopted to different social security systems and their respective aims. Thus, in countries where personal - rather than collective - responsibility is emphasized, encouragement will be given to *individuals* to arrange for personal and voluntary supplementation of the basic benefits which the State provides. Other countries, which take the view that social protection should be an entirely *national* concern, see no necessity - and leave little room - for private insurance or supplementary schemes.

Maintaining the value

Over recent decades, most countries have been caught up in what is referred to as the "inflationary spiral". Social security benefits are intended to be related to the needs of the participants of the scheme - the beneficiaries. Benefit levels, which were possibly adequate when first awarded, may no longer be sufficient - because of inflation - to buy the goods and services for which they were originally designed. A social security scheme which does not adapt its benefits to the changes in the value of money is not fulfilling its purpose. Many schemes therefore periodically revalue the benefits which are in payment, to keep them in line with the current general levels of prices or wages; indeed some of those schemes have legislative provisions which require them to do so. As long ago as 1944, the ILO was advocating that benefit levels ought to be reviewed following any substantial change in the general level of earnings or in the cost of living.

While this problem may not be so acute with short-term benefits (such as sickness benefit - where the rate of benefit is often based on very recent earnings) it is certainly so in the case of pension payments, and with old-age pensions. Typically these are based, at the outset, on past earnings which, unless themselves revalued, may reflect the level of wages paid many years ago. Unless periodic adjustments *are* made, pension values will depreciate more and more during periods of inflation.

UNIT 2: Benefits and their aims

Introduction

Passing reference has been made to some of the social security benefits; this Unit will take a more detailed look at the individual benefits which are made available under conventional social security systems.

It will be apparent that the benefits are interconnected and that all are related to the preservation or improvement of health and well-being. In the case of employment injury, sickness, invalidity, disablement and maternity benefits, the relationship is direct, for each involves total or partial incapacity for work. In the case of old-age, survivors', family and unemployment benefits, however, the relationship is not quite so obvious, but these benefits also are intended to keep beneficiaries in a state of adequate nutrition and health. There is a very specific connection between ill health and poverty and it is therefore no accident that, in a more detailed reference to benefits, the Unit begins with ...

A. Medical care benefit

What the benefit is intended to do

Medical care is provided in order to restore, improve and maintain the health of individuals. In an ideal situation, all citizens of a country would have access to medical care but such a level of provision is very expensive, the more so as modern medicine has become highly sophisticated and as this has been accompanied by peoples' increasing expectations. It is forecast that many countries will be devoting at least 10 per cent of their gross national product to medical care by the year 2000 and indeed the forecast has already been realized in a number of countries. Where, for one reason or another, the provision of medical care is inadequate, it may be necessary to make a judgement on the distribution of the country's scarce and available resources because of the many and varied demands on its finances. Not all those demands can be fully - indeed even partially - satisfied. A balance must therefore be struck between the various programmes which the State has to undertake.

Fig. 4:
*"many countries ... devoting
10% of GNP to medical care
... by 2000 ..."*

In the absence of universally available medical care provided by the State (and particularly before the days when States were able to place the same degree of emphasis on medical care as they do now) social security insurance schemes often took it upon themselves to provide some form of medical benefits - usually in the form of facilities and services - for those individuals who were participants. There are many variations in the types of scheme and benefits provided. There are schemes, for example, where consultations with doctors are sometimes provided, in addition to medicines and hospital treatment, at little or no direct charge. In others, in addition to the contribution which participants make from their income for health insurance, charges are levied for the medical services provided, or for treatment given.

Medical care systems

History has played an important part in the pattern of medical care which is presently available. Generally speaking, two broad systems have evolved and these have come to be known as the "indirect" and the "direct" systems.

Indirect systems

When social security schemes were first introduced, many countries already had well-established medical care professionals in private practice, and hospitals and similar institutions also already existed. In these situations, social security schemes tended to enter into agreements with existing services to provide facilities for insured persons, under fairly complex arrangements under which a "fee for the service" was negotiated. Prices were agreed for a long list of medical services, prescriptions, medicines, etc., and these prices were periodically reviewed.

As might be expected with this type of arrangement, difficulties can occur with regard to proper control and verification of the services provided. However, a number of devices can be used to minimize abuse; for example, operating a system where only a proportion of the fee is paid from social security itself, with the balance being paid by the insured person. In some cases the insured person is required to pay the *whole* fee and is then reimbursed, wholly or partially, by the social security office. One other variation is worth noting. A few countries use a "capitation" method of paying doctors, under which they are paid a fixed amount for the provision of general practitioner services to patients who are registered with them. All the methods mentioned above are referred to as "indirect systems".

Direct systems

With "direct" provision of medical care, it is the social security institution itself which owns, operates and controls the necessary medical facilities, and the medical staff are employed by the institution.

There are divided views as to the merits of the two systems. If the "direct" services can be provided on an efficient basis, with operational costs being adequately controlled and with a good geographical spread being achieved, this system appears to have advantages. However, the protagonists for the "indirect" system point to the "direct" system's bureaucracy, lack of free choice, loss of the important personal relationship between patient and doctor, and to the limitations in coverage of populations (since they tend to serve only the members of the particular scheme).

Qualifying conditions and duration of benefit

Many contributory social security programmes require insured persons to have a minimum number of contributions, or a minimum period of employment, before medical care benefits can be provided. Convention No. 102 indicates that there may be such a qualifying period "as may be considered necessary to preclude abuse" although it should be noted that, for employment injury benefit or maternity protection [under the Maternity Protection Convention (Revised), 1952 (No. 103)], no prior qualifying period is necessary. In practice, the conditions for entitlement vary considerably but often it will be found that countries have qualifying conditions which virtually match those for sickness benefit. Note, however, that Paragraph 4 of the ILO's Medical Care and Sickness Benefits Recommendations, 1969 (No. 134) proposes that countries should provide medical care *without* the imposition of a qualifying period of insurance or employment for *all* types of incapacity.

A limit is usually set on the duration of medical care (Convention No. 102 lays down a limit of at least 26 weeks) but there is a noticeable trend towards doing away with such limits.

The situation in developing countries

What has been said so far relates mainly to the situation in industrialized countries with well-developed social security medical care programmes but the situation in developing countries can be markedly different. Often, the population spread is very uneven, the growth rate is high, with a large proportion of inhabitants being under 15 years of age. Mortality rates, particularly of infants and children, are also high and many infectious diseases are yet to be adequately controlled. Additionally, resources are limited, there are few doctors and there is a shortage of trained personnel. From the point of view of medical care, much needs to be done and such facilities as do exist generally tend to be concentrated in urban areas.

As with other branches of social security in developing countries, medical care schemes tend to start off by covering only a limited group of employed persons, with the intention of eventual extension to other sections of the population. Some see this concentration on employed persons as a cause for adverse comment, arguing that special facilities are being provided for an already "privileged" segment of the community. There are counter-arguments, however, principally that resources are created which would not otherwise be available through public health budgets. Also, by concentrating on the health of the labour force, the productivity needed for economic growth is increased and this, in turn, will have a beneficial effect on the population as a whole.

Despite such arguments, it is certain that any system of social security medical care *must* be within the framework of the national health plan and must be developed in close coordination with the Ministry having responsibility for health (usually the Ministry of Health).

Primary health care

Any reference to medical benefits would be incomplete without mentioning the work of the World Health Organization (WHO) in the sphere of primary health care, and social security's place in this sphere. In essence, the strategy of WHO is to make the best use of available resources by employing educational, preventative and curative services to maximum advantage at village, town and regional levels. Reliance is placed on low-cost technology; for example, the supply of drugs is drawn from a model list of about 200 regarded as essential by WHO experts.

Since primary health care requires all the resources it can get, in order to achieve its goal, social security (and other sectors involved in primary health care) can contribute in a number of ways to the overall objective. Staff, equipment and premises can be shared; joint planning of financial resources (in projects such as clinic and hospital construction) can be undertaken; training can be coordinated, and so on.

The rising costs of medical care

As indicated earlier, medical care programmes are very expensive to establish and to run. Workers' organizations, as well as employers and the State, are very much concerned about the cost of programmes, particularly in the industrialized countries where costs have risen sharply in recent years. Developing countries are also beginning to feel the effects of rising expenditure, so that planners and administrators have to try to ensure that available resources are used to maximum effect.

The main reasons for increased costs are not difficult to establish, indeed some have been touched upon already. They include: better public awareness of, and general concern for, medical care; the additional and longer-term needs of expanding elderly populations; the new and costly drugs which have become available; the increasingly sophisticated (and expensive) equipment; need for highly skilled, and more highly paid, medical and other expertise which is needed to use that equipment.

In an attempt to keep expenditure down, a number of cost control measures have been introduced. These include: cost-sharing arrangements; the setting of limits on the duration of - and reimbursement for - treatment; control of the provision of drugs, or the substitution of less costly alternatives. Also, when good organization and efficient administration are coupled with effective educational and preventative measures, the average length of stays in hospital can be reduced.

B. Sickness, maternity and funeral benefits

General comments

These benefits are widely referred to as "short-term" benefits (because, as already pointed out, they are generally of short duration) and are cash benefits.

In so far as sickness is concerned, it is always hoped - and perhaps expected - that employment will normally be interrupted only for a relatively short period of time. For maternity benefits, clearly an uncomplicated pregnancy will only last for a specific period of time. Some benefit schemes allocate funeral benefit to the longer-term benefit branches of social security, but its qualifying conditions are usually minimal and fairly informal so that, when looking at how to finance funeral benefit, it is often taken into account along with the short-term benefits. It should be noted that there are two other short-term benefits, one for unemployment and one in respect of the initial incapacity following an employment injury; these will be looked at in more detail in a later section.

Where sickness is prolonged, some schemes arrange for a continuation of benefit, for example by paying invalidity benefit or, where there are complications occurring during the period of pregnancy or after childbirth, by extending the period of maternity benefit. It is usual for sickness and maternity benefits to be provided at about the same rates.

Most schemes also provide medical care in cases of maternity. If this is not given directly by the scheme itself, arrangements may be made (under special contracts) with private medical practitioners or institutions, or the facilities of public hospitals are used. In a number of countries, although it is the social security organization which pays out the cash benefits, the medical and maternity services are provided quite separately by the public health authorities.

B1. Cash sickness benefit

Before sickness benefit can be paid, certain crucial conditions must be satisfied. The first - and most obvious - is that the claimant must be suffering from an illness or disease which prevents him/her from following employment. Usually this condition is met by the provision of a medical certificate from a qualified medical practitioner but, in certain circumstances, other types of evidence of incapacity will be acceptable to the social security authorities. Medical certificates often show the period of incapacity and this - and other factors - will be taken into account when determining the duration of any benefit to be paid.

Another important condition, in a social insurance type of scheme, is that the relevant contribution conditions must be satisfied. These vary quite significantly from country to country but, where the benefit level is related to wages, they tend to require (for example) that six months of contributions have been paid since the date of the claimant's entry into the scheme - plus "X" months of contributions within the last "Y" months of employment, immediately prior to the beginning of the illness. Benefit is then related, reasonably closely, to current wages.

The *actual* level of benefit in any scheme is a matter which is decided by government or by the social security authorities. Convention No. 102 calls for minimum standards which, in a flat-rate scheme, require benefit to be pitched at "45 per cent of what a typical male unskilled labourer with a wife and two children, would receive by way of wages plus family allowances while in work; or, in a wage-related scheme, 45 per cent of wages plus family allowances for a skilled labourer".

These are relatively modest requirements and a later Convention - the Medical Care and Sickness Benefits Convention, 1969 (No. 130) - while not superseding Convention No. 102, sets *60 per cent* (instead of the 45 per cent) as the desirable standard.

In many countries the labour legislation places an obligation on employers to continue to pay wages for a certain period of time *after* the onset of an illness, and during absence from work because of (or at a certain stage during) pregnancy. Most countries coordinate their labour and social security legislation and it is increasingly common to find sickness and maternity benefits being paid by the employer to the (sick or pregnant) worker, with reimbursement subsequently being made to the employer by the social security authorities. In other schemes, sickness benefits are paid *only* when claimants have exhausted their title under the labour laws (if an initial period of sickness is financed by the employer). There are other schemes which have variations of the same theme.

Two further other points need to be made before leaving these benefits. The first is that many schemes impose a "waiting days" limitation on the payment of sickness benefit. (Convention No. 102 allows for three such days at the commencement of incapacity, to be classified as "waiting days"). The idea is mainly to save expense, since it has been shown that very brief illnesses account for a large percentage of the total claims received. The administrative cost of processing claims for very short spells of sickness is disproportionately high and therefore places a considerable demand on the contributions which are collected from participants to finance the scheme.

It is also reasoned that no appreciable hardship is caused to those individuals who occasionally go without wages during very short and intermittent illnesses. None the less, most developed schemes waive the waiting-day rule in respect of the second or any subsequent spells of illness, provided that they follow soon after a previous spell.

The second point to be made is that most schemes of the social insurance type recognize that, in a small proportion of cases, an incapacity will become chronic or prolonged. In a number of schemes, the "normal" sickness benefit period (which varies from country to country but which is commonly between six and twelve months) may be exhausted *before* the claimant has recovered; after that point, the claimant will receive invalidity benefit, if eligible. In social insurance schemes it is sometimes the case that, during a prolonged illness, title to sickness benefit is exhausted - and that there is no title to any invalidity benefit thereafter (for example, because of conditions which are attached to the duration of benefits in order to safeguard the overall finances of the scheme). In this situation, there is an obvious contradiction between social need and the maintenance of sound finances. Social assistance or general revenue financed schemes are, however, less prone to this type of problem but the levels of benefit provided will often be lower, since they are based on the criterion of hardship.

B2. *Maternity benefit*

One of the earliest Conventions to be adopted by the ILO - at its first International Labour Conference - was the Maternity Protection Convention (No. 3) of 1919. The purpose of the Convention was to attempt to ensure that a woman who was working could sustain and care for herself, and her baby, over the period before and after confinement. Today, with the increasing number of working women, it is more important than ever to make sure that conditions for a woman and her unborn baby are as tolerable as possible prior to her confinement, and that she receives proper care and support immediately after the baby is born.

Convention No. 3 has since been updated, particularly in relation to the level of benefit to be provided (i.e. not less than two-thirds of previous earnings where the scheme is wage-related social insurance) but its other principles remain largely unchanged. These are that there should be abstention from work, for example, for at least 12 weeks (starting from six weeks before the expected week of confinement) but, in any event, continuing for six weeks after the actual confinement. Medical care should be provided by a doctor or a certified midwife. Cash benefits should be available for maintenance during this period and the mother should be guaranteed reinstatement in her job. The Convention also indicates that arrangements should be made for a mother to be able to nurse her baby during working hours.

Often it will be found that a country's labour legislation requires that employers should grant paid maternity leave. Coordination between the social security authorities, labour ministries and employers is therefore essential so as to ensure there is no overlap with regard to wages and social security benefits. While the 12-week period referred to in the Convention is no doubt still the norm, a number of countries have extended the duration with respect to both leave and benefit, and have also made sickness benefits available at the end of the maternity period for the mother who has not, by that time, fully recovered from the effects of childbirth or from any complications which arose therefrom.

B3. *Funeral benefit*

Funeral benefit is one of the oldest benefits to be covered by some form of social security. The benefit is designed to help to meet the cost of burial, and associated expenses, on the death of an insured person. However, many schemes also make funeral benefit available in respect of the death of a spouse - or other immediate family member - of an insured person.

The amount of the funeral benefit varies considerably from country to country and is heavily influenced by custom. Nevertheless, the aim remains the same - that it should cover the costs of a modest, but decent, funeral. While it may, under a social insurance scheme, be a fixed amount, the amount is sometimes based on the level of old-age benefit being received at the time of death, or - in the case of death whilst in employment - the level of recent wages.

C. *Employment injury benefits and workmen's compensation*

Background

Employment injury and occupational disease programmes are perhaps the oldest - and certainly the most widespread - of all formal social security schemes. The original laws (which, in a number of countries, date back to the early nineteenth century) tended to cover only *accidents* at work and *specific types* of occupation (usually the most dangerous ones such as the coalmining, quarrying and heavy engineering industries). At the outset, the term "workmen's compensation" was used (and indeed still is to this day) to refer to the benefits paid for an incapacity which resulted from an industrial accident or disease. These benefits could be temporary or permanent, total or partial, and also included some form of death benefit.

The term "employment injury" was used in Convention No. 102 to refer to accidents at work *and* to occupational diseases, and a distinction was drawn between the different types of incapacity or disability which can flow from such injuries. Before describing these, it may be useful to take a brief look at some of the developments which gave rise to the present situation.

In the early days of the process of industrialization, employees who were injured at work could have enormous financial and other problems unless their employer was sufficiently charitable to make provision for workers on a personal basis.

Even in cases where it was possible to take an employer to court, for redress for an injury which arose in the workplace, the problems associated with producing adequate evidence and the necessary proof were almost insuperable for workers or their survivors.

A means therefore had to be found of avoiding - or at least reducing - the litigation process, which at that time was weighted heavily against the worker. A rough and ready way to do this was to require that the owner of the enterprise (in which the injury incurred) should provide compensation in prescribed cases - without *any* question being raised as to whether the injury was attributable to fault on the part of the employer, the employee, or any third party.

Today, the general trend is towards placing employment injury within social insurance programmes. Indeed, in some countries, there has been a widening of the whole concept of compensation for accidents to include not only those which occurred in the workplace but also those which took place outside, at home or in the street - in other words, whether work related or not.

Fig. 5:
" ... the general trend ... placing employment injury within social insurance programmes"

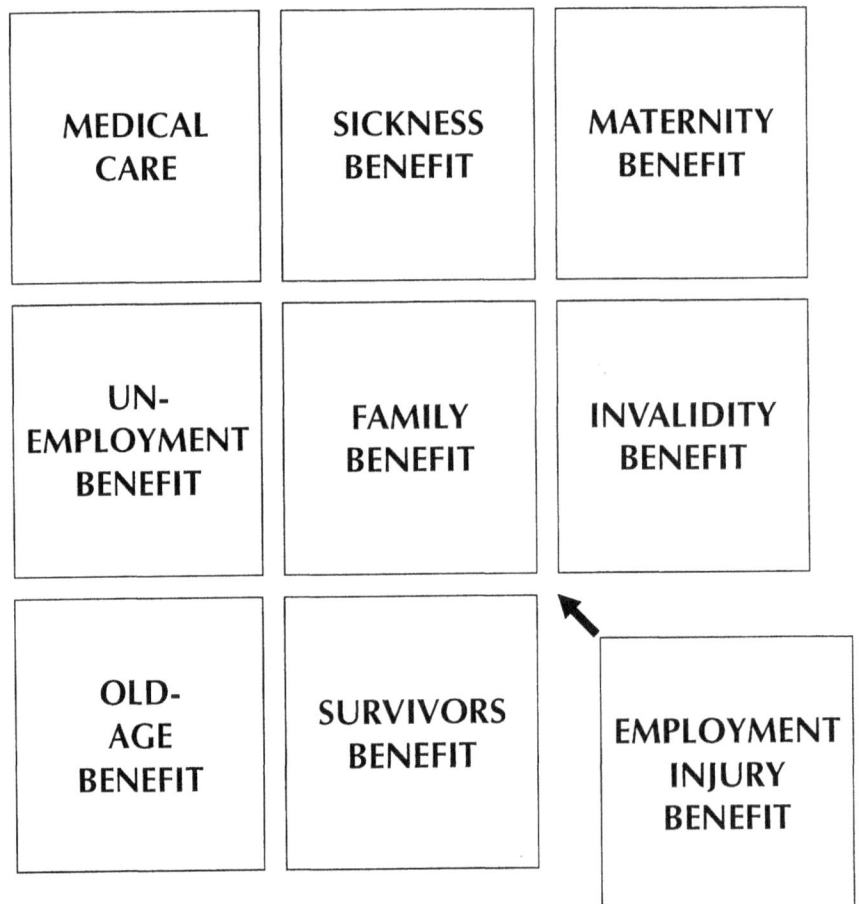

MEDICAL CARE	SICKNESS BENEFIT	MATERNITY BENEFIT
UN-EMPLOYMENT BENEFIT	FAMILY BENEFIT	INVALIDITY BENEFIT
OLD-AGE BENEFIT	SURVIVORS BENEFIT	EMPLOYMENT INJURY BENEFIT

C1. Workmen's compensation

Initially, workmen's compensation was a legal liability, placed on employers, to provide compensation in certain regulated situations. Employers could, in most cases, either take this liability on charge themselves or take out some form of commercial insurance to cover the legal liability and, in a number of countries, the law made it compulsory to do so.

The levels and duration of compensation varied - and still vary - widely from country to country. Typically, however, there are five elements in the compensation structure. These are:

- medical care and hospital treatment;

- benefits in respect of temporary incapacity;

- a lump sum for permanent and total incapacity;

- a percentage lump sum or grant for a permanent but partial incapacity; and

- a sum, usually a lump sum, where death has occurred.

Workmen's compensation schemes have stood the test of time and have been refined and extended to deal with many of the difficult problems surrounding employment injuries. However, critics point to two weaknesses to be found in the majority of schemes. The first is that disputed claims must go before the courts; this causes delays in settlement, employer-worker confrontation, and acrimony - which often results from such proceedings. Additionally, pressure may be exerted on the worker to accept what, at first sight, may appear to be an attractive settlement but which, in reality, may not correspond to his or her long-term financial situation or physical handicap. A further weakness is that, even in very serious cases of employment injury or in the case of death, many schemes do not provide periodical payments or pensions.

Lump-sum payments to "settle" outstanding claims *may* be justified in certain circumstances but, generally, they are markedly inferior to a pension for the worker who is faced with lifelong disablement, or for the survivors.

To these should be added another possible deficiency. Where employers are *not* compulsorily required to insure their liability with an outside private or public carrier, a heavy lump-sum settlement (in favour of an injured or deceased worker) could well create substantial financial problems for them. Employers who are unable to meet their liabilities may find that proceedings are undertaken against them for recovery. It is then possible that, as a result, they will be put out of business and the worker or survivor(s) would then get little or nothing by way of recompense.

Coverage

As already indicated, workmen's compensation schemes did not cover all employees from the outset; even today, many still do not. Opinions vary on whether, for example, non-manual workers (particularly those who are quite highly paid) should be included in such schemes. Frequently in the "fringe areas" of the employed population there is no coverage; examples include the domestic service sector, and sectors where the status of an employee is difficult to define, as is frequently the case where relatives are working in a family business.

In social insurance programmes the increasing tendency is to cover *all* employees. However, some problems do arise in the "fringe" sectors, as with workmen's compensation schemes.

C2. *Employment injury insurance-contingencies and benefits*

Two international labour Conventions are of interest and importance when looking at employment injury benefits and the related conditions: Convention No. 102, and the Employment Injury Benefits Convention, 1964 (No. 121). In an employment injury insurance scheme, benefit is paid from a common fund and provides for: medical care; the interruption of earnings because of incapacity following an injury; the "residual loss of physical or mental capacity"; and for cases of fatal injury.

It is important to establish whether and in what circumstances a work accident occurred, or whether a particular disease is an occupational disease caused by the worker's exposure to conditions at work and which brought it about. A "work accident" or "occupational disease" is usually defined in the appropriate legislation which will also require that the accident must have occurred - or the disease developed - "in the course of employment".

One of the advantages of bringing employment injury cover under a "social insurance umbrella" is that contestation between the parties concerned is reduced. As shown earlier, under workmen's compensation schemes, an employer - or the insurance company with whom the employer has insured the liability - has an interest in narrowing the interpretation of a work accident and this can cause delay, litigation, undue expense, as well as the possibility of souring the relationship between employer and worker.

Fig. 6:
"... Contestation between the parties ... is reduced."

Medical care

As with other benefits provided by employment injury programmes, medical care provisions tend to be more liberal than those provided by other branches of social insurance. The reasons for this are mainly historical and many would argue that there is no longer any justification for such a distinction to be made. Under Convention No. 121, an injured worker is entitled to every type of care, without limit of time, and does not have to meet any of the costs.

Interruption of earnings

In workmen's compensation schemes, a distinction is often made between temporary and permanent incapacity for work, i.e. whether the injury or disease is likely to last only for a short period or will lead to permanent incapacity. Normally, under employment injury insurance schemes, this distinction is of no consequence, since benefit is paid for incapacity for work following from the accident (or development of occupational disease) for as long as that incapacity lasts. The rate of benefit is often higher than for sickness benefit; indeed Convention No. 121 mentions a minimum of 60 per cent of pre-accident earnings and many countries exceed this minimum figure.

So long as incapacity for work continues, most schemes continue to pay the benefit on a periodic basis. After a specific period (usually between six and twelve months) the vast proportion of injury cases, with the requisite medical care, will have cleared themselves up, or the worker's condition will have stabilized. At this point most schemes arrange for a medical examination to determine the extent of the impairment to the worker - referred to as "the residual loss of faculty".

Residual loss of faculty

Determining the residual loss of faculty can be very difficult. The Conventions refer to "loss of earning capacity likely to be permanent, or corresponding loss of faculty" but, in practice, it is almost impossible to make an evaluation which is absolutely correct because of the different circumstances which affect individuals, e.g. employment prospects, psychological factors, etc.. In some countries the legislation includes a list of physical injuries and the related loss of faculty; this method is of particular use in countries which have limited medical resources. Other countries attempt to assess the extent of the disability in terms of the resultant loss of earnings, taking into account the pre-injury status of the person concerned, rehabilitation, and future career prospects.

Total incapacity attracts an award of benefit at the 100 per cent rate; lower levels of disablement will give title to an award which is proportional to the full benefit. Relatively small assessments (perhaps when disablement or impairment is assessed at between 10 and 30 per cent) generally attract a lump sum payment rather than the periodic pensions paid in respect of the higher assessments. ILO Recommendation No. 121 suggests that lump sums should be paid only in cases where the disablement or impairment does not exceed 25 per cent.

The methods of arriving at awards which are as fair as possible vary considerably from country to country and are influenced not only by policy requirements but also by the availability and adequacy of medical and administrative expertise. The aim, however, must always be to compensate for the loss which has resulted from the work-related injury or disease. Many schemes make special efforts to rehabilitate injured persons by retraining them and providing useful alternative work. Where someone is so seriously handicapped that they require the constant attendance of another person, a special allowance is often paid and, in some programmes, an unemployability supplement may also be paid.

Survivors' benefits

When an employment injury results in death, pensions or grants are paid to survivors. The legislation defines "survivor" and (once again, for historical reasons) the scope tends to be rather wider than for survivors under the non-employment injury branches of social insurance schemes. Priority is given first to the widow and then to children of the deceased. Widowers may also receive benefit but usually this is only where they relied, for their maintenance, on the earnings of the deceased spouse when she was alive. Dependent parents can also benefit in certain circumstances, as may other dependants, if the total amount of benefit which is available under the legislation has not already been allocated to higher-priority survivors. Typical rates for survivors' pensions are 30 per cent of the worker's pre-accident earnings for a surviving spouse; 15 per cent for each child (20 per cent if both parents are dead) and 20 per cent for a parent; with the overall total being subject to a maximum of, perhaps, 75 per cent.

Prevention of employment injuries

Workers' organizations attach particular importance to safety in the workplace, as indeed do most employers' organizations. The health of the individual worker depends on a good industrial environment. Social policy must be directed towards the goal of reducing accidents and injuries and, in many countries, standards of conduct and safety have been established which both workers and employers are required to respect. Indeed social security benefits themselves are at the end of the protection chain but it would obviously be desirable for them to be unnecessary - which would clearly be the case if accidents and diseases could be avoided. The economic, domestic and social distress caused by accidents and diseases does not need to be emphasized.

Social security institutions usually cooperate closely with those agencies which are concerned with industrial safety, health, and welfare, and there are some social security institutions which, themselves, undertake the necessary policing exercises or which divert funds to enable this to be done. One way in which employment injury benefit branches have helped to draw attention to the vital importance of safety in the workplace is to penalize those employers whose safety record is poor. This is done by requiring them to pay higher employment injury contributions; i.e. they are "rated" according to their accident history. In this way, an attempt is made to encourage employers to pay greater attention to their safety record by "hitting them where it hurts" - in the pocket. Trade unions have been very active in the field of accident prevention and do a great deal to train workers and to make them more aware of their responsibilities.

Accidents happen not only in the workplace, however, but also in the street, in the home and elsewhere, and there is a growing level of concern about the overall effects of accidents of all types. Many would argue that the needs of an injured or disabled person are exactly the same whether the handicap is work related, non-occupational in origin, or congenital. There is a movement in some countries towards removing the special benefits, for those who are injured or disabled at work, in favour of a common and uniform approach.

D. Old-age benefits

The various types of programme

Most countries now have some form of social security programme for old-age protection which covers, if not all the population, at least sectors of it. There are a variety of schemes, spread over the various social security programme structures, and these include flat-rate pensions, employment related pensions, means-tested non-contributory pensions, and sums payable at specific ages under provident funds. Occupational (employer-based) pensions and private (personal) insurance pension plans are also being linked to some state systems.

The extent to which the population is covered by a pension scheme depends largely on two factors: the age or "maturity" of the social protection system and the stage of industrialization which has been reached. Both scope and coverage are also considerably influenced by historical, cultural and social patterns.

Despite the large number of countries which have introduced social security legislation in respect of old-age cash benefits, there remain some which, for many different reasons, have still not found it possible to do so. The economy may not be able to support a programme - at least for the time being - because emphasis has to be given to other priority areas. In some cases the need has not yet been recognized or indeed may not yet be pronounced. For example, societies which retain strong extended family ties tend to take care of their elderly as a matter of course, and the need for old-age benefits may not be so urgent or apparent. Even in those countries, however, there is often a limited old-age benefit programme for certain groups (e.g. civil servants and public employees) with the idea that similar programmes for other sectors of the community will be introduced gradually "when the time is right".

A closer look at some types of programme for old-age benefits will reveal different and important characteristics.

1. *Universal benefit schemes.*
   In principle, universal schemes cover *all* residents, and provide pensions for all those over a certain age, whether working or not and irrespective of income. Often the only condition attached to the receipt of the benefit, apart from the age condition, is that the person must be a long-term resident or a citizen of the country. Benefits tend to be paid on a flat-rate basis, i.e. at the same rate for everyone.

2. *Social assistance schemes.*
   These schemes, which provide means-tested benefits including old-age benefits, may either provide benefits "as of right" or supplement the benefits received under other programmes when these do not cover the person concerned, or where they provide insufficient minimum income. The social assistance scheme may also stand on its own, that is to say it may be the sole general social protection measure. Often the benefits rates are set at subsistence levels.

3. *Social insurance schemes.*
   Old-age and other benefits are provided to participants subject to their work record or the contributions they have paid during their working lives. Benefits may be earnings-related or paid on a flat-rate basis, or a combination of both.

4. *Provident funds.*
    These generally provide lump sums at a specified age. The lump sum is made up of the accumulated employer and worker contributions to the fund, with added interest. In some schemes it is possible to convert the lump sum into a continuing periodic pension.

5. *Private pension schemes.*
    These are not, strictly speaking, part of the social security umbrella. However, some governments are now working alongside employers' occupational schemes and private personal pensions providers so as to arrange an alternative form of additional benefit in old age. One way of doing this is to permit individuals to "opt out" of certain parts of the State's old-age scheme, provided that the employer-based (or private) pension plan, which the individual is covered by, satisfies certain prescribed conditions - as happens in the United Kingdom. It goes without saying that the best old-age benefit is the one which continues for the remainder of the recipient's life and it needs to be a regular, continuous pension (though subject to review in the case of social assistance schemes, if the resources of the recipient increase). Ideally the pension should be sufficient to meet the needs of the pensioner and be revalued whenever there is an increase in the cost of living.

Contingencies and pensionable ages

Working capacity generally diminishes with advancing age and most societies accept that there comes a time when an individual has earned the right not only to rest but also to be provided with resources sufficient to live in a reasonable manner. Some occupations are dangerous, or entail hard physical labour, and there are those who take the view that workers in such occupations have earned the right to an earlier respite than those whose work appears less onerous. Thus, there are a number of different views as to what constitutes the "normal pensionable age".

Given the choice, some people will want to continue to work; others are relieved when the time comes for them to retire from their normal occupation. Nevertheless, whatever the individual's view, whatever the type of scheme in operation, the fact remains that the "normal age" for receiving old-age benefit is that which is established by the legislation.

Fig. 7:
"... Given the choice ...
some ... want ... to work ...
others are relieved ...
to retire ..."

With universal schemes, old-age benefit is put into payment when the specified age is reached, and this was the practice with the early social insurance schemes. Social assistance means-tested schemes provide old-age benefits *only* if the person concerned meets the prescribed income conditions. Since provident funds are forms of compulsory savings schemes, the accumulated amount standing to the credit of the participant is paid out when the age specified in the rules is reached. The regulations governing the payment of employer-based (occupational) pensions, and of private pension plans, also stipulate the age for the payment.

Retirement

There is some controversy as to whether or not a person who continues to work *after* the normal pensionable age should be allowed to receive an old-age benefit. As pointed out earlier, in social assistance (means-tested) schemes, benefit is payable *only* if income is below a certain limit and in such schemes, therefore, the situation is quite clear.

For other types of scheme, however, there are those who take the view that, since old-age pension is intended to be an income replacement measure, it should not be paid until income does need replacing - i.e. when retirement *actually* takes place.

Others take the view that, since the contribution requirements (in a social insurance scheme) and residence conditions (in an universal scheme) have been satisfied, there should be an *unconditional* right to receive the benefit when the stipulated age is reached - regardless of whether the individual stops work or not.

Between these two points of view are to be found a number of "intermediate" arrangements. For example, in some schemes, the retirement benefit is suspended until work actually ceases but accumulation of additional benefit continues during the period between normal retirement age and cessation of work. Another method is to pay a reduced old-age benefit, along with wages, after the normal retirement age is reached. It is usual, however, to put old-age benefit into payment at a relatively advanced age (e.g. age 70) *irrespective* of whether or not the individual continues to work thereafter.

Another factor which may influence the decision, on the age from which old-age benefits should become payable, is the country's financial and economic climate. Where, for example, government policy is to encourage older workers to remain in the labour force it may be that, if the payment of benefit was made conditional on cessation of work (i.e. on "retirement"), this would constitute a disincentive to continue at work - since people would no doubt want to retire in order to obtain their pensions. Old-age benefits are costly, particularly so in countries where a decline in the population's younger workers is accompanied by an ever increasing number of elderly - because of greater longevity.

This point will be revisited later in the section which deals with the financing of social security.

Normal pensionable age

The legislation for most schemes defines a "pensionable age". At this age, provided that all the other qualifying conditions are satisfied, old-age benefit (by whatever name it is referred to) is usually put into payment. In some schemes, "normal pensionable age" is the same for men *and* women but there are still many schemes where the pensionable age for women is five - or even more - years lower than for men. However, even in some of those schemes, for example in the United Kingdom and Switzerland, the process of gradually bringing the pensionable age for men and women into line has already begun.

In the majority of schemes, old-age benefits become payable between the ages of 60 and 65 years, but there are countries which enable "length of service" pensions to be put into payment on completion of a certain period of employment, which is commonly between 30 and 40 years.

"What should be regarded as normal pensionable age?" This has become a major policy question in recent years and, understandably, there is much public pressure for a reduction. There are a number of reasons or factors which prompt that pressure, including: job dissatisfaction; fatigue; inability to adapt to technological and other changes. At the same time, however, there are those who take the view that being forced to leave fulfilling employment, simply because of pension rule requirements, is most unsatisfactory. In some countries there is a move towards greater flexibility in pension policies. In the United States, for example, the statutory pensionable age will be increased from the present age of 65 to 67 by the year 2027.

Despite the fact that changes are taking place in a number of schemes, the fact remains that once a "normal pension age" is accepted and introduced it is very difficult to change it - particularly to increase it. It must also be remembered that changes in the pensionable age have financial implications - pensions have to be paid for. *Lowering* the normal pensionable age will clearly *increase* benefit expenditure considerably and create a burden which might be regarded as insupportable.

A number of countries make special arrangements to pay early old-age benefits to those who have worked in arduous or unhealthy conditions, even where the individuals are not in poor health. Special schemes have been set up in several countries for miners, the police, the military, and the merchant marine service, which recognize the onerous nature of the work performed. Advancing age is more prone to bring complete or partial inability to continue in employment, because of health problems, because of redundancy, or through extended unemployment, and a number of schemes coordinate their old-age pension arrangements with the invalidity or unemployment programmes. In some countries, the view is taken that early retirement of older people should be encouraged (or that a strict retirement policy should be enforced) on the basis that this will result in more jobs being available for the young unemployed.

Other modifications of the "normal pensionable age" include voluntary early retirement, and deferment of retirement whereby the individual will qualify for a higher rate of pension either on eventual retirement or on reaching an upper age limit, at which the pension is paid irrespective of whether or not work continues.

In the industrialized countries, arrangements often exist which are designed to lessen the psychological impact of retirement. Loss of the discipline of regular employment, and of companionship formed over a working life, can be distressing for some when they are suddenly removed from the work environment. Recognition of this has led to a policy of preparing individuals for retirement by giving them special concessions during the run-up to retirement age. For example, pre-retirees might be allowed to reduce their actual working hours on a phased basis, or additional leave might be granted to ease the transition into retirement. In Scandinavian countries, Spain, and Germany, partial old-age pensions may be facilitated in the years prior to the formal pension age. These pensions provide some replacement of the lost income which results from the reduced working time.

Qualification for old-age benefits

Reference has already been made to the fact that conditions for benefit differ, depending upon the type of old-age benefit scheme in operation. In a universal scheme, for example, it is only necessary to prove age and residence. In a social assistance means-tested scheme, there will be an additional test - the need to show that income is less than a specified level. In a social insurance scheme, individuals must show that they have participated in the scheme for a certain period of time by paying contributions or proving employment, as well as having reached the pensionable age.

These tests are necessary for two reasons. Firstly, they prevent people who have made only minimal contributions to an insurance scheme from procuring a pension. In the case of universal or social assistance measures, they prevent people from migrating to a country purely for the purpose of taking advantage of the scheme in operation. Secondly, the tests establish some form of relationship between the contributions, or the employment period, and the benefits which have to be paid; this financial aspect is most important.

There is a great diversity of minimum periods of coverage required to qualify for an old-age pension. Social insurance systems often require payment of contributions for a *minimum* of ten or 15 years before a pension can be paid. Convention No. 102 and a later Convention, No. 128, (Invalidity, Old-Age and Survivors' Benefits Convention, 1967) provide that a reduced rate of benefit should normally be made available where a person has completed 15 years of contributions or employment, but there are schemes under which the amount of benefit varies according to the duration of the contributions, employment, or residence, with no minimum qualifying period being required.

When a pension scheme is first introduced, it is often the practice to make special concessions to older people who, because of their age, would not otherwise be able to meet the minimum qualifying conditions. Special "credited" periods of contributions or employment are usually granted to help them meet the conditions in order to receive old-age benefit.

When employment is interrupted by periods of sickness, maternity, unemployment, etc., for which benefit is paid, it is common to find special arrangements for the crediting of contributions (or employment periods) for the period during which it is paid. This prevents a "contribution gap" in the qualifying period and assists the ultimate satisfaction of the qualifying conditions for old-age benefit.

Methods of payment

In most countries, old-age benefits are paid in the form of a pension, i.e. a periodic payment - which may be weekly, monthly, or even quarterly. Social insurance pensions are often wage related - with the amount of pension payable being determined by the level of wages earned over the "service" life of the individual. Another way of relating pensions to earnings is to base the pension on an average of the wages earned in the final years of work. In this way the pension has some relationship to the standard of living which the claimant enjoyed immediately prior to pensionable age. With both these approaches, the earnings figures used are often revalued to take account of the changes in the value of money.

Universal and social assistance schemes, however, generally provide flat-rate pensions and the amount is based on the country's subsistence cost of living (often referred to as the "poverty line"). Some social insurance schemes have also adopted this method but they are usually supplemented by earnings-related (or contribution-related) complementary schemes - on a national, sectoral, or enterprise basis.

It is difficult to make a direct comparison of the pension amounts provided in different countries but the ILO has attempted to provide an indication of what an average wage earner might expect to receive, by way of pension, as a fraction of his or her earnings. Conventions 102 and 128 require that, normally, it should be not less than 40 per cent (Convention No. 102) or 45 per cent (Convention No. 128) of average wages, where there have been 30 years of contributions/ employment under a social insurance scheme, or where there have been 20 years of residence under a social assistance or universal scheme.

Maintaining the value of a pension

Inflation can play havoc with pensions, as with other sectors of a country's economy. Pensioners are more vulnerable than wage earners to the immediate effects of increases in the cost of food, goods, and services, and it is therefore important that they be able to benefit from any general improvement in living standards. For these reasons, many countries have a mechanism for adjusting pension rates from time to time. However, it cannot be claimed that such mechanisms always work perfectly.

The adjustment of new pensions, and pensions already in payment, may be based on different criteria. Some countries have regard to the movement of a consumer price index while others take account of changes in the average wages of the working population. Yet others look at both of these criteria before deciding what adjustment, if any, should be made.

There are three main methods for dealing with adjustments. The first is to legislate for automatic adjustment; the second is to provide for a periodic review but without setting absolute amounts; lastly, there is the system of "ad hoc" adjustments.

Population and ageing

The figures relating to the age spread in country populations is of interest and concern when related to pension plans. There are countries where the average population is very young - for example, where as many as half the population is under 20 years of age. Conversely there are countries - in particular, a number of industrialized countries - where the statistics show that older people are beginning to outnumber younger ones.

Both these trends have important repercussions for benefit schemes. With a young population, the problem is often to create sufficient jobs for them all. Countries with an ageing population, with many people already receiving pensions - or expecting to receive them when they reach pensionable age - face expenditure on pensions which is bound to increase substantially because of the high number of pensioners, even without taking into account possible inflation. Furthermore, people are living longer and, given the steady increase in the number of the elderly, the cost of medical care and social services will inevitably also increase.

Whichever social security system is in operation, without "full funding" of the country's pension scheme it is the active sector which supports the non-active; the working population supporting the retired. As the numbers in the active sector decline - particularly in industrialized countries - succeeding generations of pensioners, in the years after 2000, may well be forced to accept lower standards. This problem has been exercising the minds of social planners worldwide and a number of ideas have been developed in an attempt to deal with it. These include raising the pensionable age and making individuals more responsible for their own financial protection in their old age.

E. Survivors' benefit

Introduction

In the context of a social security scheme, "survivors" might be expected to refer only to widows and children. Although the majority of survivors *do* fall into those categories, the change in lifestyles and patterns of family life require that, if social security systems are to move with the times, they must reflect the new situations.

There are many societies in which it is common for both partners of a marriage, or of a stable union, to be working. Very often both parents will be out at work or, increasingly, it may be that the woman is the family's major provider. Many countries also have an increasing number of single-parent families.

National schemes therefore need to reflect the wide differences in culture and tradition, with regard to dependants, within the immediate or the extended family. In countries where polygamous relationships are accepted, different criteria will clearly need to be adopted to the dependency status of survivors than will be the case in countries where monogamy is the norm.

It is therefore not possible to refer to a "typical" survivor's benefit scheme. However, it is possible to draw attention to the major features of some of the systems which are in operation, beginning with the "widow"* - since this is likely to be the principal beneficiary in most schemes, especially so in countries where tradition dictates that women should not work outside the home.

---

* Throughout the manual, whenever reference is made to "widow", it should be remembered that, in a number of countries, no distinction is drawn between a woman who is legally married and one who has lived in an extra-marital relationship - provided that stability of relationship can be proved.

Qualifying conditions for survivors' benefit

In a social insurance scheme, the qualifying conditions are usually satisfied automatically if an old-age pension was in payment at the time of death. Thus, if a male pensioner dies and leaves a widow, provided that the widow is not herself in receipt of an old-age pension by virtue of her own contribution or employment record, the test for a survivor's benefit will be satisfied. Given that death of the participant can occur *before* pension age has been reached, there are different and much shorter qualifying periods in these circumstances.

Conventions 102 and 128 indicate that, in general, the prescribed person (the person on whose record the survivors' benefit is based) must have five years of contributions or employment but, in practice, there are considerable variations amongst survivors' schemes with some having far more generous conditions attached to them.

Beneficiaries

National social security legislation will always take the surviving widow as the principal beneficiary in the first instance, though some legislation then varies the extent of the benefit, having regard to the family situation. A widow having care of her late husband's children will usually expect to have social security support while the family grows up. Most schemes also have regard to a widow's state of health so that, if she is relatively elderly or is otherwise unable to support herself, she will receive a periodic pension. In a number of schemes, however, a young widow without children will receive benefit only for a relatively short period because she will then be expected (or encouraged, perhaps through training or retraining) to take up work.

Protection of the child is an obvious feature of survivors' benefit schemes, though it should be noted that, where a country has a scheme of family allowances, coordination is necessary between the paying authorities (or the different branches of programmes) to ensure that there is adequate, but not excessive, protection. National legislation normally defines "child" for benefit purposes. Issue children (generally those born to one or both partners and living with the insured person at the time of death) would obviously be included but sometimes the definition is broadened to include illegitimate or adopted children. This enables account to be taken of *who* actually supports the child and moves beyond the strictly legal "property and inheritance" questions. Many schemes provide cover for children - through survivors' benefit - until they leave school, although children who are invalids are often covered for life.

A number of schemes also have regard to other surviving dependants although few go outside the immediate family circle. Aged dependent parents are sometimes included, as are other persons who relied on the deceased breadwinner for support.

Despite the range of provisions for survivors, it is not possible to provide *all* social security provisions from the scheme's survivors' benefit branch. Other branches also need to play their part, particularly those relating to family allowances, invalidity benefits, social assistance and health services.

With different family compositions and the variety of relationships and types of dependency, ingenuity and flexibility is required on the part of planners and administrators if they are to respond adequately to the changing social needs.

Survivors' Benefits

Conventions No. 102 (Minimum Standards) and No. 128 (Invalidity, Old-Age and Survivors' Convention, 1967) indicate that the minimum rate of benefit for

- a widow with two children,

- after 15 years of contributions or employment (or ten years of residence) should be the same as the old-age pension rate for a married couple.

  This would mean that a widow would receive *one half* of her late husband's old-age (or invalidity) pension entitlement, while *one quarter* would be provided in respect of *each* child. However, the proportions vary greatly between countries, with widows receiving pensions (having regard to age and family responsibilities) ranging from 40 to 100 per cent of the deceased husband's entitlement.

Many schemes make distinctions between "half-orphans" (children who have lost one parent) and "full-orphans" (those who have lost both their parents). Where schemes do make this distinction, the full orphan is usually awarded twice as much benefit as the half-orphan, and the rules for benefit seek to ensure that the payments are used for the benefit of the children.

Additional comments

Some additional points need to be made. First, the programmes which provide survivors' benefits following death (of a covered person) which results from an employment injury should not be confused with those applying to death from natural (or non-occupational) causes. In the former case there is no contribution or residence test and benefits are often, for historical reasons, set at a higher level.

Second, it is difficult to make direct comparisons between different schemes relating to survivors' benefits, because it is also necessary to take into account benefits and services which are often provided to widows and dependent children through other programmes.

The third and final point relates to the changing family situations which were referred to previously. Some survivors' benefit programmes recognize the fact that it may have been the wife who was the economic provider in the family, so that if she dies the husband and children should receive some form of protection similar to the widows' and children's benefits in traditional schemes. While Convention No. 102 covers widows only, and Recommendation No. 131 advocates equality for widowers who are "invalid" and "dependent", these concepts are increasingly being questioned - particularly in European countries where constitutional courts are beginning to rule out distinctions in survivorship cases based on sex. There is increasing recognition, too, that a dependant (perhaps a sister, brother, son or daughter) may have had to stay at home to look after someone who had been the breadwinner in the family and, therefore, that he or she should also have the benefit of social security protection.

F. Invalidity benefit

What is meant by invalidity?

Looking at the laws of different countries will reveal a number of different definitions of the social security contingency referred to as "invalidity". The variations will be influenced by the concept which is followed and the concepts can be presented as follows.

- *Physical invalidity*
  ... the total or partial loss of any part of the body, or of any mental or physical capacity - but irrespective of the economic or occupational consequences of that loss.

- *Occupational invalidity*
  ... the loss of earning capacity resulting from inability to follow the occupation previously undertaken by the person concerned.

- *General invalidity*
  ... the loss of earning capacity resulting from inability to find a suitable job, even jobs which might mean a change in the work previously undertaken as well as, perhaps, some sacrifice of status.

The essential difference between them is that, in the first case, emphasis is put on impairment *without* taking into account its economic consequences for the victim, while both the other concepts give the *economic aspects* of invalidity much greater weight. In practice, however, the legal definition tends to take both features into consideration so that an assessment of the disability has regard to the physical *and* the economic consequences, though almost all countries require a specified minimum degree of disability for there to be title to benefit.

However, it is not quite so simple for, in some countries, invalidity has come to be thought of as simply "an extension" of normal sickness - and invalidity benefit as a form of "prolonged sickness benefit". There are also countries where it is regarded as a form of "premature old-age benefit" and where older persons, who have not yet reached the official pension age, can obtain benefit on the grounds that they are unable to follow employment because they are wholly or partially incapacitated. A relatively new phenomenon, coupled with the downturn in the economy in a number of countries, is that sympathetic consideration is sometimes given to the possibility of making invalidity benefit available to elderly persons who have no jobs to go to, who cannot be retrained, or who cannot be expected to relocate to places where jobs might be found.

Generally, however, invalidity benefit is regarded as one of the "long-term" benefits and is grouped alongside old-age and survivors' benefits, with the same basic qualifying conditions - at least in a social insurance scheme. This was the grouping used in the ILO Convention No. 102 and the feature was also carried over into the later 1967 Convention (No. 128). Invalidity benefits are usually available in countries which have social assistance or the universal benefit type of scheme, while statutory provident funds normally pay out the due balance of funds once the participant's invalidity is established.

Assessment of invalidity/ disability

Most social security schemes rely, in the first place, on medical evidence provided by a doctor indicating that the scheme member concerned - the invalidity benefit claimant - is unable to work because of some mental or physical condition. The procedure which then follows depends on the scope of the particular scheme and whether or not other specified conditions are satisfied. The claimant may be required to appear before medical assessors in order to identify the problem more precisely, and to obtain a second opinion about the extent of the invalidity and its probable future course. Also at this time, the possibility of vocational rehabilitation may need to be investigated since it is desirable that, where possible, the claimant is encouraged to follow some useful occupation. He or she might, for example, no longer be able to follow the previous occupation or to work regularly but, with help, could undertake some less demanding work.

Fig. 8:
"... the claimant may ... need to be medically assessed ..."

When entitlement is being considered, some laws require that a comparison be made between the health condition of the claimant and a "normal" person of the same age and sex, remembering that age is often a significant factor because the same impairments and health problems will usually have more serious consequences for the elderly than for the young. This is usually reflected in the award that is ultimately made.

The term "invalidity" usually implies a reasonably stable incapacity, that the invalid's condition is permanent in nature, and is unlikely to change. Indeed many national laws emphasize the permanent nature of invalidity, with benefit *only* being awarded if the authorities are satisfied that the condition will not improve. Even so, some countries permit revisions of the initial assessment and also require beneficiaries to submit themselves for periodic medical examinations to see whether the condition (for which invalidity benefit is being paid) has improved or deteriorated; consequent readjustments are then made to the level of benefit, as appropriate.

Qualifying periods

In social insurance programmes, as with old-age and survivors' benefits, invalidity benefit is usually subject to qualifying periods (either a certain number of contributions or intervals of employment). In universal or social assistance schemes it is usually subject to periods of residence. Qualifying periods of this kind are necessary in order to prevent abuse of the scheme by those who might otherwise obtain a long-term (and potentially very expensive) benefit at short notice. They also ensure that there is a significant participation in the scheme, by the individual concerned, before benefit becomes available.

Qualifying periods vary considerably from scheme to scheme. The relevant ILO Conventions refer to 15 years of contributions or employment, and 10 years of residence, for a standard invalidity benefit, with a reduced rate being available after five years of contributions, employment, or residence. When all working people are members of a *contributory* scheme, the Conventions lay down that benefit should be payable after only *three* such years.

However, there are some schemes which provide invalidity benefit without *any* conditions - other than that the applicant is a member of the scheme - or which regard invalidity benefit as an extension of sickness benefit (as mentioned previously). Other schemes may have shorter qualifying periods for younger members than for older ones; yet others treat invalidity which results from non-work related accidents on the same footing as occupational accidents and therefore waive qualifying periods.

Benefits

As shown already, there are countries which require that there is *total* and *permanent* invalidity before benefit is awarded. At the other end of the scale there are many schemes that assess the extent of *partial* invalidity and/or the consequent loss of earnings and pay a proportionate pension. Usually an invalidity benefit for total disability will be calculated on the basis of the claimant's average earnings over a period prior to the onset of invalidity - often the 12 months immediately preceding the onset.

In a social security programme of the social assistance type, the award of invalidity benefit will be subject to a means test and this is also the case with some universal schemes. In all types of programme - except for provident funds - increases in respect of dependants are usually available, as are various supplements and additions for particular problems (such as blindness, the need for constant attendance, etc.).

It will be apparent that provisions for invalidity benefit can be quite complex and, in many countries, awards which are made are not always straightforward. It has already been pointed out that invalidity benefit may be used to try and ease the problems associated with unemployment in cases where it is impossible for older persons to find suitable alternative work. In instances where individuals have worked for many years in dangerous occupations, or where their work has involved heavy manual labour, there are schemes under which an invalidity benefit may be more readily available during the years preceding the statutory pensionable age - indeed where it is almost regarded as a form of premature old-age pension.

Rehabilitation

It is in everyone's interest to have adequate rehabilitation services for those who are handicapped. In some countries it is the social security authorities who are responsible for the establishment and support of such services. In others, the general responsibility will rest with the social services or may be contained in separate enactments dealing with national health services, education, housing, etc.. Sometimes no distinction is made as to the cause of the impairment; for example, someone who is injured - whether at work, in the street or at home - will still be provided with the same services as someone who qualifies for invalidity benefit under the social insurance programme.

The rehabilitation services may be responsible for the care, the training and the employment of handicapped persons and will also, perhaps, deal with special services for the blind, with the education and welfare of handicapped children, with disabled ex-servicemen and women, etc..

Convention No. 128 of 1967 requires that every member State which ratifies the Convention should provide for rehabilitation services which, wherever possible, help disabled people to resume their previous activity or try to find them suitable alternative gainful employment. Some countries have been able to set up special sheltered workplaces and provide subsistence allowances, transport, necessary tools and equipment, and even loans and grants, to individuals who are undertaking vocational rehabilitation. All these facilities are designed to assist a disabled person to live as full, as useful, as fulfilling and as active a life as possible.

In addition to the overriding, morale-boosting, aspect of such programmes, it obviously helps the finances of any social security programme if the handicapped can rely on their own resources rather than exclusively on the State's. To this end, there are a number of schemes which regularly monitor invalidity - and work-disabled - pensioners to ensure that they are taking full advantage of services provided by the programme itself or which may be available to them from some other source.

G. Unemployment benefit

The contingency

Social security unemployment benefit schemes are commonly found in industrialized countries, which have market economies, but only rarely in countries with large rural, agricultural-based communities. Unemployment benefit is paid to those individuals who, through no fault of their own, have become unemployed and who, as a result, have lost the earnings on which they and their families depended. When the unemployment is "involuntary" (that is, where individuals have done nothing to cause themselves to be out of work) benefit is paid - but usually only for a relatively short period of time. The problem of restricting the period is not, however, a simple one. Unless there is fairly strict control over potential claimants, the social security authorities will find that there is an open-ended commitment to paying benefit. This might also be accompanied by the danger of reducing - or even removing - the motivation to find other work.

The different approaches

Because of those problems, and others related to the adequacy of financing and the difficulties of administering unemployment benefit, only 63 countries* around the world have been able to establish such schemes. Three types of scheme can be identified:

- Compulsory unemployment insurance - in which specified categories of workers must participate.

- Subsidized voluntary unemployment insurance - where participation is optional (except, perhaps, in the case of trade union members who are required to subscribe to union funds).

- Unemployment assistance - where public funds are made available to those out of work, on condition that a means test, income or earnings test, is satisfied.

---

* Source: *Social security throughout the world;* Social Security Administration, Washington DC 20008, USA. ISBN 0-16-048224-0.

In about half of the countries with an unemployment insurance scheme, it *is* compulsory and is often a branch of the main social insurance scheme. In some of those schemes, unemployment assistance may also be available as a form of "safety net" measure, where a person has exhausted the right to insurance benefit or fails to satisfy the insurance benefit conditions.

Because of recent economic changes, especially in the industrialized countries (with the decline of traditional basic industries and the restructuring of others like shipbuilding, coalmining, steel making, railways, etc.) there have been attempts to make some programmes more flexible, seeking to provide *partial* benefits where earnings have been reduced because of work-sharing or retraining programmes, or because of shortage of work due to lack of orders or bad weather conditions.

Labour (or other types of) legislation often obliges employers to make severance or redundancy payments to workers who are discharged for reasons *other than* misconduct. Normally such payments are made as a lump sum and bear some relationship to the length of a worker's employment. Where no unemployment benefit scheme is in operation, these payments at least provide a "cushion" during the interval between work periods. Opinions differ as to whether they can be regarded as a form of unemployment protection. There are those who argue that severance or redundancy payments are, in effect, forms of deferred pay or compulsory savings which are related to the work and should not, therefore, be taken into account when determining title to any unemployment benefit which may be available. Others argue that, since both redundancy/severance pay and unemployment benefit arise from the same contingency - the loss of a job - the employer should not be expected to double the expense by contributing towards funds to cover both payments.

Who is protected by unemployment benefit ?

Unemployment benefit schemes normally protect only those who are in regular paid work since - so the theory goes - it is only those people who are at risk of involuntary unemployment. Thus, the self-employed are not usually covered, nor are persons who undertake casual or occasional work. Additionally, there are major administrative difficulties in proving unemployment benefit for those groups, not least the problems of identifying those involved, determining earnings and collecting the appropriate contributions.

Some schemes extend protection to *all* sectors of the wage-earning community, regardless of whether they have weekly wages or monthly salaries and whether in the private or the public sector. If a person is in receipt of some other social security benefit (for example sickness benefit) unemployment benefit will be denied to them on the grounds that they already have some form of income replacement.

Qualifying conditions

As might be expected, the payment of benefit is usually subject to the satisfaction of certain conditions. Although the *conditions* are often quite complex, the *objective* is quite straightforward - to make sure that benefit is paid *only* to those who rely on regular paid work for their livelihood and who have become *involuntarily* unemployed.

Under insurance schemes, a suitable qualifying period of regular work must have been undertaken prior to the start of unemployment; in other words, sufficient contributions must have been paid, or employment must have lasted, for a required minimum duration. The reason is simply to ensure that the claimant is properly within the scope of the scheme; many schemes requiring a minimum period of six months, perhaps in the 52 weeks immediately prior to unemployment.

In unemployment assistance schemes, where benefit depends on a means test, it will normally be necessary to show that the individual has been resident in the country for a given (minimum) length of time.

A number of other tests are frequently applied. It was pointed out in the section dealing with claims to sickness benefit that, as well as satisfying the contribution, employment or residence duration tests, it is also necessary to show that the person concerned is genuinely "incapable" of work by reason of sickness. In the case of unemployment benefit, in addition to satisfying the contribution or work/residence tests, at least five other issues are normally considered.

- First, the question of whether the claimant left work voluntarily or not. Where workers leave work merely because of dissatisfaction with the job, or on a mere whim because they know they can simply rely on unemployment benefit, the underlying objective of the benefit is defeated. Although it is sometimes difficult to establish exactly what the justification was for leaving work, a critical look is nevertheless taken at the circumstances.

- The second question concerns discharge for alleged misconduct and many unemployment benefit schemes disqualify workers (at least for a specific length of time) who have been dismissed for this reason. This is another question which is often difficult to resolve and legislation sometimes attempts to spell out exactly what is regarded as "industrial misconduct". (For example, it may include repeated negligence, theft, intoxication at work, wilful disobedience, frequent unjustified absences, etc.).

- Third is the question of industrial disputes and work stoppages. Social security schemes need to remain neutral and workers are usually disqualified from receiving unemployment benefit where the unemployment results directly from an industrial dispute. Problems arise, however, in cases where a particular worker is *not* a party to the dispute, or where workers are unable to follow their employment because of the closure of the workplace, even though they may be willing to work. National practices vary greatly in the way in which these difficult issues are dealt with.

- A fourth aspect is that a claimant must be "willing, capable and available" for work. This means that, within reason, the claimant must remain part of the active labour force. Once again, the condition gives rise to problems and a number of schemes try to be flexible, for example, when considering the question of whether a person who is in doubtful health is *actually* available for, or even capable of, full-time work. Usually there will be some coordination with other social security branches, or with authorities responsible for vocational training or rehabilitation.

- The fifth aspect to be considered is the question of "suitability for the job" and, as with the four previous questions, this also poses a number of problems. The fear of being disqualified from receiving benefit may encourage individuals to accept work which is quite unsuitable for them. Age, previous experience, past wages, the location of the new job, will all - ideally - be taken into account but, over recent years, other considerations have become increasingly important; for example, the state of the labour market and the length of time during which the individual remains unemployed.

It will be apparent that these are all complex issues which can make it difficult to take a totally objective view when determining title to unemployment benefit. It is not surprising, perhaps, that disputes arise and in an attempt to ease some of these a number of devices have been tried, including the submission of problem cases to some form of appeal or industrial tribunal and the establishment of (uniformly applied) case law.

The benefits

In social insurance programmes, the usual rates of unemployment benefit are approximately 50 to 60 per cent of previous earnings. Occasionally the benefit may be at a flat-rate, normally in schemes where unemployment benefit is of the social assistance means-tested type. Supplements for dependants are usually also payable. Convention No. 102 prescribes that unemployment benefit should be at the rate of 45 per cent of the claimant's previous earnings (for a man with a wife and two children) taking family allowances into account. In the case of a flat-rate scheme, the level should be 45 per cent of an unskilled worker's wages, again taking family allowances into account.

The same Convention expects that unemployment benefits should be paid for at least 13 weeks, during the course of a one-year period (26 weeks in the case of social assistance) but schemes vary considerably with regard to the duration of benefit. Most, however, apply some form of waiting period before benefits commence, commonly between three and seven days.

As already indicated, the more well-developed schemes are often closely integrated with other social security branches. While the principal objective is to pay benefits to the covered person, the scheme may be used as an integral part of an overall policy directed at promoting employment or facilitating training or retraining.

Some recent trends

Those policies - the promotion of employment and the emphasis on vocational training - have changed the traditional role which unemployment benefits have played in social security protection in recent years, particularly in industrialized countries with market economies. Some countries have introduced special arrangements to help school-leavers, have assisted self-employed persons who have lost their livelihood, have actively encouraged the unemployed to learn new skills, have provided grants for them to set up their own businesses, and have paid out special allowances to stimulate mobility. Subsidies have been given to employers to be used as a part of the wages of new worker trainees and money has been made available to enterprises to prevent or minimize retrenchment and redundancies. In some instances it is the unemployment benefit schemes themselves which have found the necessary finance for these costly exercises; in others, the finance has been provided from the general revenues of the State or has been raised through levies of one type or another.

The provision of unemployment benefit cannot, however, solve the root problems; these require an overall and comprehensive policy which is designed to stimulate the economy. Unemployment benefit can nevertheless play a useful role in alleviating hardship and encouraging the unemployed, by retraining and other measures, to obtain · suitable employment elsewhere.

Developing countries

Much has been done to minimize the scourge of unemployment in industrialized countries, which have the advantage of working from a relatively sophisticated base. However, countries which are still in the course of development are in a particularly difficult situation. The overriding priority, in most developing countries, is to promote employment and there has often been a lively and sometimes bitter debate over whether some form of income protection can be introduced for unemployed people.

A frequent argument *against* the possibility of introducing some form of unemployment protection is that, given the lack of resources (and such resources as are available in developing countries have to be allocated across many fronts) the priorities for expenditure must be concentrated elsewhere, for the time being. In any event, the establishment of *any* form of unemployment benefit programme must be preceded by a properly organized network of efficient employment offices, and for the most part these do not exist. Any realistic unemployment benefit programme will certainly outrun the resources of any contributory scheme. It would also be very unfair to provide the small, comparatively privileged, wage-earning sector with unemployment benefits which are denied to the mass of their fellow citizens - who are unable to take up wage employment because of the lack of opportunity.

H. Family benefit

General comments

Another of the branches of social security deals with allowances for families. Convention No. 102 (1952) incorporates the main ideas contained in a 1944 instrument, the "Income Security Recommendation, No. 67", which had indicated, quite simply, that family benefits should be for the "responsibility for the maintenance of children".

Family benefits are, in fact, somewhat different from the other cash benefits provided by social security programmes. Whereas those programmes seek, in principle, to provide income when wages are lost or interrupted, or when a person no longer works on account of old age, family benefits are normally paid *along* with wages and recognize the fact that wages do not usually reflect family commitments.

Fig. 9:
"... family benefits ... normally paid along with wages ... which do not usually reflect family commitments

Family benefits were introduced later than other branches of social security for a number of reasons. One was the prevailing idea that large families and poverty went hand in hand and that, because of the expense involved in raising children, this could provoke an eventual decline in population numbers unless some special encouragement was given to parents by helping with the costs.

The growing concern over the general welfare provisions for children also resulted in the introduction of other reforms. Thus, over the years, many countries have adopted policies for free education, subsidized meals, and school medical services. In yet other countries, when accommodation is being allocated, priority is given to families with children. Income tax arrangements invariably provide special concessions and allowances, taking into account the number and ages of a taxpayer's dependent children.

The different types of family allowance

Two types of family allowance can be distinguished: those which are referred to as "employment-related" and those provided under a national "public service" arrangement.

Employment-related allowances were made available in the early 1920s, in Belgium and France, by industrial employers who were worried about the increasing pressure for higher wages. They decided to organize "equalization funds" in an attempt to even out the cost, per worker, of supplementing wages proportionate to the size of a worker's family. This is, of course, an application of the insurance principle. Today, allowances (at a flat rate for each qualifying child) tend to be paid along with the worker's wages with the account being subsequently settled with the institution running the family allowance or benefit scheme.

There are many variations on this theme, with some countries having special arrangements for self-employed workers and with the State paying a subvention from its general revenues, so that, in the most advanced examples, schemes have more or less the same scope as alternative national public service arrangements.

Public service, or universal programmes, also began in the 1920s. In New Zealand, allowances were first made available to families with small incomes but this practice was soon dropped and, today, those countries which have universal schemes usually provide them irrespective of parental income, financing them from general State revenues. There is no direct link between family benefit and employment and it is important to note that the benefit is normally paid to the mother. The emphasis is on help towards the family budget and in many instances, the allowances increase for second or subsequent children.

Family composition

Title to family benefits depends on a number of factors. These tend to vary between countries, though most family benefit schemes do follow Convention (102) and pay in respect of each child. Universal schemes tended, at one time, to exclude the first child in each family on the grounds that "normal family income" should be sufficient to meet the cost of one child and, if the State were to help, this might in some way undermine parental responsibility.

Country legislation usually defines the term "child", for the purposes of family benefits. This is necessary because, in other respects, children may be excluded (for example, under inheritance laws, etc.). Issue children and stepchildren will no doubt be included, and legally adopted and illegitimate children also. The test is often that the child or children are living with and/or are maintained by the parent or guardian, but no hard and fast rule can be given.

Age is also a factor. Many countries tie the upper age limit, for title to family benefits, to the school-leaving age (commonly 14 to 16 years) but the limit may be extended if the child continues further education, undergoes vocational training, or becomes an apprentice. Invalid children also retain title until they are absorbed into some other scheme which pays comparable - or better - benefits.

While some schemes make "progressive" amounts of benefit available (one amount for the first child, a greater amount for the second child, etc.) employment-related family benefits usually make no distinction. It should also be noted that, in some countries, family benefit schemes are directly linked to national family policies; increases (or decreases) in benefits may well be used as an instrument for encouraging (or discouraging) the number of children in a family.

Other family benefits

The definition of "family" and "child", contained in the legislation relating to family benefits, is frequently also used for other social security benefits, for example when establishing title to survivors' benefits in respect of children, or where dependency allowances are added to basic sickness benefits or personal old-age pensions. There is also an affinity with maternity benefit. Some family benefit schemes make prenatal and birth grants available. They may also be the vehicle for paying marriage grants and housing allowances, and holiday bonuses are a feature of some schemes. New developments in family benefits continue to take place, for example supplementing benefits when a parent, who normally works, stays at home to care for a child (up to a certain age) or to look after a sick child.

There are still many countries, however, which have not yet been able to introduce a family benefit scheme or where, for the time being, they are considered inappropriate. Interestingly, in 1940, only seven countries had full family allowance programmes. That number increased progressively until 1977 when 65 programmes were in operation; in 1995, the number had further increased to 88*.

Rates of allowances

It is particularly difficult to make comparisons, between countries, of the effective value of allowances. Too many factors are involved - such as real exchange rates, cost of living, and the different types of benefit included in the respective programmes. The impact of taxation must also be taken into account for, in many countries, the levy of a direct tax on personal incomes may affect, or be affected by, the payment of family benefits. The combination of cash benefits and services, and the national or local policies applied in the fiscal sphere, are such complicating features that a rate cannot be defined in the same way as for other social security benefits. For this reason, all that Convention No. 102 could do when attempting to deal with this aspect was to ask ratifying countries to ensure that, where a scheme is universal in application, it should provide a benefit at least equivalent to 1.5 per cent of an unskilled worker's wage, multiplied by the total number of children of all residents; if the programme is limited in coverage the figure should be 3 per cent of an unskilled worker's wage, multiplied by the total number of children covered.

Benefits in kind

Before leaving family benefits, reference should be made to some of the other services which are often provided to assist families. In some countries these are quite extensive, although they are not necessarily regarded as part of the social security programme package. Labour legislation and other laws often incorporate welfare facilities for expectant and nursing mothers. Free or subsidized milk and meals, the provision of medical care, assisted holidays, are also a part of some school (or other) programmes. Concessionary housing may be available and special medical attention is often given to expectant and nursing mothers and to any children who are not yet within the school system.

---

*Source: *Social security throughout the world*; Social Security Administration, Washington DC 20008, USA. ISBN 0-16-048224-0.

SOCIAL SECURITY PRINCIPLES

MODULE 4:
FINANCING SOCIAL SECURITY

International Labour Office - Geneva

MODULE CONTENTS

UNIT 1:   **Financing implications for social security**

Introductory comments

    A.   Factors affecting costs and trends

    B.   Systems of financing

    C.   Fixing the level of contributions

    D.   Investment of reserve funds

    E.   Particular aspects of costs

UNIT 2:   **Social security and the national economy**

Introductory comments

    A.   Social security and income distribution

    B.   The economy and social security contributions

    C.   Savings and investment

    D.   Economic pressure and social security

MODULE 4

FINANCING SOCIAL SECURITY

UNIT 1: Financial implications for social security

Introductory comments

Tis topic is dealt with in detail in a manual in this series entitled SOCIAL SECURITY FINANCING (Number 3 in the series)*. This module will therefore only briefly examine the subject.

Social security benefits are expensive and they have to be paid for. People need to have confidence that benefits will be available when they are required and, to this end, there must be an effective administration and the money to meet the payments which are needed.

How are benefits financed and what problems are associated with financing social security? A proper appreciation of these aspects will give a better insight into why it is necessary to concentrate resources in this or that particular area and, when allocating resources, to determine the priorities. Schemes cannot be introduced without very careful attention to their financing and when a new scheme is being developed it is essential to cost the proposed benefits to ensure that they can be afforded. This applies to almost all types of scheme, whether a small and simple occupational pension scheme or a national insurance or means-tested scheme.

The only exception to this general rule is provident funds for, as mentioned in an earlier section, the combined contributions of employers and workers are collected and made available at some future date. Even with provident funds, however, the question arises as to how big a contribution can be tolerated if it is not to adversely effect a worker's take-home pay and the ability to meet daily expenses or, from an employer's point of view, to affect the profitability of the business and thus the ability to keep the workers in employment.

* *SOCIAL SECURITY FINANCING - ILO Geneva - ISBN 92-2-110736-1*

In industrialized countries, criticisms are often made about the rising cost of social security and the progressive extension of schemes. There are also those who believe that social security has not altogether fulfilled its social purpose. In developing countries, social security is usually criticized because it is not sufficiently comprehensive or because it is seen as providing for those who are already comparatively privileged at the expense of those whose needs are just as great but whom it fails to cover. Despite such criticisms - some justified, some not - the achievements of social security cannot be minimized and it must surely be regarded as one of the most fundamental and beneficial developments of the twentieth century.

In industrialized countries, social security developments are very much reflected in the growth of expenditure. For example, some countries in the European Community are spending up to one-third of their gross domestic product on social security. This is a price which many people, particularly the younger generation, complain about when paying their contributions or social security taxes whilst, at the same time, taking it for granted that payment is necessary. Few people consider what they would do and how they would manage financially if they themselves had to bear the full cost of raising a family, of supporting parents, and meeting - whether fully or in part - the health care costs of elderly relatives.

It is important to emphasize that point, for a price *has* to be paid for the extensive social protection which citizens in industrialized countries receive and it is most relevant to any discussion about social security financing. Those who are involved in the shaping of social policies must constantly bear the cost factor in mind.

Fig. 10:
"... a price has to be paid for ... extensive social protection ..."

A. Factors affecting costs and trends

Since different countries have their own inherent characteristics, direct comparisons between them are not always practicable. Whilst one country may have an age distribution of the population in which a large percentage of its citizens are over a particular age - perhaps older than 50 - others may have a very young average population, many of whom are of school age, or of working age but unable to find work. Such factors have an obvious effect on the financing of social security, as do the types of economic activity undertaken, and the various levels of earnings.

The incidence of the short term benefit contingencies can be reasonably foreseen; it is therefore relatively easy to estimate the cost of these benefits and this is done on a fairly short-term basis. However, the long-term benefits - together with disablement benefits under employment injury schemes - are in a different category. They are obviously more expensive, in many cases being paid month by month until the beneficiary dies. It is rather more difficult, therefore, to produce accurate estimates of the prospective cost of such benefits, even where accurate data is held about the age and sex distribution of the population at risk. Provision must also be made for present pensioners. It might be thought that it would be sufficient to ensure that each person, when in the workforce, pays an adequate contribution in one form or another to meet the cost of his or her ultimate benefit; this financial device is referred to as the "full funding" of benefits. Unfortunately , however, it is not quite so simple.

In the period of time during which prospective pensioners are building up their title to long-term social security benefits, many changes may take place. Wages may alter radically; inflation may soar; existing pensioners may have their pensions increased; perhaps, because of inflation, such increases may be well beyond any forecasts made at the commencement of the scheme. These factors, and others, must be taken into account in the actuarial and financial evaluations which need to be undertaken, on a regular basis, to determine the present and future costs of the scheme.

Actuarial forecasts are particularly important in the case of insurance-based social security schemes but, in principle, the same sort of exercise must be undertaken for all systems whether insurance, universal or means tested. Various adjustments can be made if the costs of a scheme are too high, for example by reshaping the qualifying conditions for benefits, by directing resources into other areas, by reviewing priorities, etc..

B. Systems of financing

The "fully funded" system, referred to earlier, is relevant to private pension schemes but is not applied to social security schemes. A comparable approach for social security schemes is referred to as the "general average premium" system, which at the outset determines a constant rate of resources as a percentage of the insured wage bill. In theory, this guarantees the perpetual financial well-being of the scheme. At the opposite end of the scale are the "annual assessment" or "pay-as-you-go" systems in which, broadly speaking, the annual income and expenditure are the same.

In practice, an intermediate, partially funded system is generally used in which some capital is accumulated, not for expenditure, but for the interest which it yields. One system used is referred to as the "scaled premium" where the contribution rate remains stable over successive intervals of time, being revised only when the accumulated reserve fund starts to be depleted.

Mention should also be made of the "assessment of constituent capital" system, which is generally used to finance pensions under employment injury branches of social insurance. Under this system, calculations are made to equate each year's income with the capital value of pensions awarded in that year; therefore each year's contribution receipts - invested, with interest - should in theory be sufficient to meet the liabilities arising from all awards made in that year.

C. Fixing the level of contributions

In the case of universal or means-tested schemes, the benefits are financed from the general revenues of the country which come, for the most part, from the various sources of taxation. The amount of money allocated to meet the cost of social security benefits will be estimated, having regard to anticipated expenditure, and will then be approved by Parliament.

In the case of social insurance schemes, contributions are normally paid by insured persons and by employers, sometimes with a state subsidy taken from general revenues. As pointed out previously, the contributions may be uniform for all insured persons ("flat-rate") or they may be earnings related.

It should be noted that, when contributions are paid at a flat rate, benefits are also usually payable at flat rates. This approach is an easy one to understand but one of its problems is that a contribution which is at the same proportion of earnings for *all* insured persons bears most heavily on the lower paid. For this reason, some schemes which are referred to as "flat-rate" in fact reduce the contribution where earnings are low - yet maintain the benefit levels if these do not exceed the worker's normal earnings.

There are two methods of fixing the appropriate rate of earnings-related contributions. With the first, contributions are strictly proportionate to earnings. With the second, contributors are divided into wage bands, and earnings within each band attract their own flat-rate contribution. Often an upper limit, or "ceiling", is set for benefit *and* contribution purposes. These limits, or ceilings, are revised from time to time, in line with the movement of economic indicators (price rises, cost of living indices, inflation, etc.).

D. *Investment of reserve funds*

Any institution which collects money will accumulate funds, especially with certain types of financing methods. It is normal financial practice to invest monies which are not immediately required and to obtain the best possible returns. This is also the case with social security schemes.

The basic principles governing the investment of social security funds are the classic ones of safety, yield and liquidity: *safety*, in order to ensure that contributors' funds are maintained; *yield* in order to maximize the funds (and thereby perhaps to keep contributions lower, or to increase benefits); *liquidity* in order to ensure that the necessary money is on hand when needed.

An additional factor - social and economic utility - is usually also considered when the prerequisites of safety, yield and liquidity have been met. The idea behind this is that social security funds should, to the extent possible, be invested in order to improve the overall quality of life in the country. This may take the form of investment in housing, health and education, or in enterprises that are creating jobs. Normally, however, any funds which are available for these types of project are invested through the appropriate financial institutions, otherwise the focus of the management of social security schemes might well be diverted from its primary objective - to ensure the efficient operation of the scheme.

E. Particular aspects of costs

Two other aspects, mentioned only briefly so far, have far-reaching consequences on overall costs and thus on the financing of social security. These have been, and continue to be, the subject of considerable concern and debate.

The first is the soaring cost of old-age pensions. In industrialized countries, the cost is increasing because of the continuing maturity of schemes (i.e. more and more people having satisfied the qualifying contribution/employment/residence conditions and receiving benefits); because people are now tending to live longer; and because of the age at which the pensionable age has been set. Almost all countries have a "normal" pensionable age, established when schemes were first set up. Some critics believe that the time has come to review that age, and attention continues to be given to the best strategy for raising it, or perhaps for making it much more flexible, so that those who are capable of working beyond the "normal pension age" - and who wish to - should be allowed to do so. It goes without saying that raising the pensionable age would have very significant effects on the overall cost of social security.

Arguments for raising pension age are countered, however, by the assertion that releasing older workers improves the chances of young unemployed people to find jobs; also that after, perhaps, 40 years of work, older persons certainly deserve a paid respite.

The second area of concern is the increasing cost of health care. In developing countries, there are obvious difficulties in finding sufficient money to set up and deliver health care on a nationwide basis. There are many demands on the available money and services, and other priorities may have to be established. In industrialized countries also, priorities for available resources have to be set. Progress in medicine has not led to either a fall in the frequency of illnesses or a reduction in the use of health care services. People have more sophisticated expectations and are more aware of, and concerned about, their health than their parents were. It is natural for patients to want to take advantage of new and expensive technologies if they think these may bring a cure. Additionally, as people live longer, their need for access to medical care and social services increases; and more attention is given to the special needs of the seriously disabled, whose chances of survival are now far greater than before.

UNIT 2: Social security and the national economy

Introductory comments

It has already been seen that social security can have a profound impact on the economy of a country, particularly so if the scope of the programme is extensive. An earlier section pointed out that social security, in its present state, developed out of the growth of industry, the shift of populations from rural to urban setting, and the increasing use of cash in the economy. Workers who had been used to rural subsistence, within their villages or extended families, became totally reliant on money wages after moving into the towns. With this change in the economic setting, some kind of formal social security programme became vital to protect workers against the risks which menaced regular incomes and which threatened the ability to support themselves and their families.

Social security programmes are still a crucial element in industrialization, economic development and growth - though the form which programmes take clearly depends on priorities. The contents of these programmes help to determine the direction and pace of economic development to a significant degree. Social security may be used - deliberately so - as an instrument for economic change, as already mentioned in the sections dealing with social security benefits.

Medical care helps to provide a fit and efficient workforce, thus affecting productivity and, consequently, economic growth. Cash benefits replace wages during unemployment, absence due to work injuries or illness, or when women have children. People can move from place to place more readily since benefit rights do not depend on continuing employment with the same employer. The longer term benefits provide the means for continuing purchasing power and thereby assist in the circulation of money. Investing surplus funds in insurance or provident fund schemes can make important contributions to the availability of finance for social and economic purposes.

A. Social security and income redistribution

The broad *social* aim and effect of social security programmes is to improve the quality of life; the broad *economic* aim and effect is to redistribute income. Under social security, income is redistributed in two ways; by *horizontal* redistribution, and by *vertical* redistribution.

Horizontal redistribution means that taxes or contributions paid on a regular and continuous basis are then transferred to those for whom the system provides. In other words, the working, healthy population who do not, at least for the time being, need social security benefits, transfer resources to those who do require such benefits. When the social security programme is a small one (for example a limited scheme covering only a small segment of the population) the horizontal transfer may be fairly insignificant but, where there is countrywide coverage, the scale of transfer can be considerable.

A provident fund scheme does not transfer income in the same way or with the same impact since, as explained previously, the fund is a form of individual savings plan - albeit of a compulsory nature. Some redistribution is, however, achieved by way of the transfer of the employer's element of the combined contribution to the benefit of the worker.

Vertical redistribution is effected by transferring money from higher-income groups to those with smaller incomes, something which is now done almost as a matter of course by governments. Taxes on incomes, and controls on prices, wages and profits, are some of the direct means of achieving vertical redistribution: indirectly such transfers can be effected by applying certain types of policy to, for example, education, housing projects, health and child welfare, as well as through social security.

The level of social security contributions in an insurance scheme can be weighted, for example in favour of the lower-paid workers, and this is a part of the mechanism for vertical redistribution. Benefits can also form part of the mechanism and many schemes give preferential treatment to the lower-paid worker by making the conditions for - and the amounts of - benefit (particularly old-age or invalidity benefits) especially favourable to them.

B. The economy and social security contributions

As mentioned already, some critics of social security say that, in many countries, "social" charges - of which social security contributions form a part - have become exorbitant, are a drain on the economy, and that the burden of social costs is damaging to economic progress.

Undoubtedly the imposition of, or an increase in, social security contributions does have an impact which filters through the economy. Usually the effect on workers' wages has meant not so much a drop in consumer demand and spending, but pressure for wage increases. However, it is the *combined effect* of contributions and benefits which must be considered. Contributions are raised to meet increases in benefits and the money provided by the benefits returns through the economy. Certainly, when times are hard, less is spent on luxury goods but, none the less, social security benefits go some way towards protecting the purchasing power for essential goods and foodstuffs and helps to maintain the circulation of money.

In industrialized countries, where the number of pensioners has risen dramatically over recent decades, so has their social and economic influence. The total amount of their disposable incomes has increased and, on the whole, they are consumers rather than savers. Again, therefore, the effect is not damaging to economic prosperity.

The social security contribution of the worker, in economic terms, is relatively straightforward; it is an element of wages, of take-home pay. The status of the employer's contribution is more complex, since it forms part of a package of costs, profits, prices, wages, turnover and taxes. While the increase in a worker's contributions can, for example, be measured in terms of "a drink or two a week", the same increase in the employer's contributions can amount, globally, to a considerable sum and perhaps have an untoward impact, particularly in labour-intensive enterprises.

Different views can thus be adopted on the effect of social security costs on production and employment. While benefits are generally spent to meet current needs, there are those who argue that the *volume* of benefits (particularly family benefits and old-age pensions) sustains *heightened* demand for goods and services - and thus stimulates employment. Others argue that benefit *costs* reduce the profitability of an enterprise and encourage employers to substitute capital-intensive systems for labour-intensive systems.

Perhaps a reasonable way of looking at the issue is to appreciate that social security represents only a *part* of total labour costs - albeit a significant part - and to take the philosophical view that economic and social well-being are mutually sustaining.

C. Savings and investment

Social insurance and provident fund schemes can generate and accumulate considerable financial surpluses. The amount and nature of these surpluses depend on the scheme and the method of financing applied but they must, of course, be used in some way; normally they are invested to produce the best possible return.

Many developing countries have accumulated significant surpluses. This is either because they have a national provident fund (essentially a savings scheme) or because they introduced old-age benefit branches to their social insurance systems at a time when the average age of the population was so low that most participants would not qualify for benefit for at least a generation. The result, in each case, is the availability of a considerable surplus of funds.

Generally the national legislation lays down the way in which surplus funds should be invested. This is often in government securities or under the direction of an investment committee on which central government is strongly represented. Perhaps it is surprising, therefore, that in a number of developing countries, although the national authorities may rely on funds generated by their social security schemes as an important source of funds for capital formation and investment, social security is not always integrated with development planning.

Unfortunately, developing countries often face particular problems when confronted with where and how to invest surplus funds. There is a good case for devising, and insisting on, public policies which are designed to safeguard the adequacy of returns on social security investments and to preserve the real value of funds - but where do these countries find suitable investment opportunities which match up to the desirable criteria?

D. Economic pressure and social security

In recent years most countries have felt the effect of economic strain, some much more than others, and it is widely acknowledged that there is no single, overall solution. When planning or reviewing the finances of social security measures, policy makers and actuaries take account of predictable changes and make assumptions on the basis of population statistics and economic expectations. Safety margins *are* left but, in times of economic crisis when inflation is high and there is a recession with consequent widespread unemployment, severe strains are placed on all forms of financing, including that of social security.

With social security schemes which are based on insurance principles, benefit levels can match earnings levels when the contribution is a proportion of the wage and, provided that wages follow the inflation rate, the result may not be catastrophic. However, in countries with a flat-rate contribution and flat-rate benefit structure, there may be a need for frequent changes in the standard contributions in order to pay for increased flat-rate benefits.

It is standard practice, in a number of countries, to finance social security from general revenues. The governments of those countries are constantly involved in the setting of priorities and allocation of funds, even more so when the taxable capacity is strained following economic difficulties. At such times there are strong competing claims on the available resources. It should also be noted that the closer a contributory social security programme approaches complete coverage of the population, the more it can be likened to a universal scheme and the more the contributions approximate to a general tax - with similar effects on the economy.

Reference has already been made to the problems resulting from demographic changes. The economic implications for some industrialized countries, of an increasing older age group within the population, means that, in years to come, if there are no dramatic changes, only one or two active workers will be supporting one old-age pensioner - a ratio which will have intolerable consequences.

Fig. 11:
"... if there are no dramatic changes ... one or two active workers will ... support ... one old-age pensioner ..."

Important implications also arise from the increasing number of working women, from the phenomenon of single-parent families, from the insatiable need for health services - to mention only a few. The problems of financing social security in industrialized countries may well be viewed by developing countries with something less than enthusiasm. Nevertheless, they can profit from these experiences by planning and implementing programmes which are best suited to their particular economic conditions.

Despite the difficulties, however, social security programmes have been, and continue to be, of immeasurable benefit to the vast majority of people and are a bulwark against social unrest. There is, of course, a price to be paid and it is undoubtedly necessary to have regard to what is generally acceptable. It is also necessary to monitor continually, to review and adapt programmes so that they respond to prevailing situations and inevitable changes and yet, at the same time, attempt to give the best value for the money spent. This brings us naturally to the administration of social security.

SOCIAL SECURITY PRINCIPLES

MODULE 5:
HOW SOCIAL SECURITY
IS ADMINISTERED

International Labour Office - Geneva

MODULE CONTENTS

MODULE 5

HOW SOCIAL SECURITY IS ADMINISTERED

UNIT 1: Administrative structures

Introduction

As the administration of social security schemes is also dealt with in detail in a separate manual in this series - ADMINISTRATION OF SOCIAL SECURITY (Manual number 2)* - this module will take a relatively brief look at the topic.

In developing countries, a better understanding of what social security can achieve, even with a limited spread of coverage, may encourage greater initiatives to be taken by both workers and employers to press for further improvements in the scope of new or existing social security programmes. Hopefully, this Manual will add to that understanding by drawing upon the experiences of a variety of countries and their social security schemes, by pointing to some of the advantages and also to some of the potential pitfalls of the different approaches to social security.

This Manual, together with others in the series, will go some way to showing what happens to the social security contributions and taxes paid by workers and employers. Additionally, when considering some of the organizational and administrative aspects of social security, the manuals may help to explain why there is a need for the direct involvement of workers and employers in social security programmes, for example by representatives from workers' organizations and employers' associations, who may be asked to serve on social security appeal tribunals, or who may become members of statutory boards set up to direct and deliver social security programmes.

ADMINISTRATION OF SOCIAL SECURITY ILO Geneva - ISBN 92-2-110735-3

It should not be forgotten that workers and employers have a primary interest in the prevention of the contingencies referred to in this Manual. It is far better to proactively spend time, effort and money, on avoidance of the contingencies where possible (for example by preventing accidents and injuries at work, by preventing sickness or invalidity, etc.) than to pay benefits when such contingencies arise.

Social security must continually adapt itself to the changing world and to changing needs. Social security schemes have to face many challenges and overcome many problems and the ILO is constantly attempting to contribute to a better understanding of them. To take one example, the study which lead to the production of *Into the twenty first century: The development of social security* (ILO Geneva, 1984) brought together a group of eminent social security experts to examine evolving social security developments. The publication provides valuable insights into the difficulties facing social security, its future role and the developments which are likely to take place. In one way or another, workers and employers alike have a vital part to play in social security programmes, as those programmes affect almost everyone - whether directly or indirectly.

In looking at social security administration - what should be expected of it? Any administration exists for one purpose only - to provide an effective and efficient service to its clients. In the social security context, the clients are the various participants in the scheme, viz workers and employers, and - if the programme is so designed - other sectors of the population such as the self-employed and the non-employed.

The ideal administration is one which is both effective *and* efficient, working along with its participants, providing help and advice. Since there are rules and regulations which need to be observed, the administration *must* apply them *impartially*. There should be a clear-cut right of appeal, if a decision goes against a claimant or a beneficiary, to an independent appeals body.

These are the ideals but, unfortunately, in practice they are not always met. Few, if any, institutions can claim that there is no room for improvement in the running of their administrations.

A. *Structure and organization*

There is no particular or special model for social security administrative structures and organization. Different structures suit different situations and tend to have developed on the basis of what was regarded as right at the time - and then adapted as required.

In the countries where near-universal coverage has been achieved, the structural pattern is usually quite formal and it is common to find a single institution responsible for all aspects of the programme - from collection of contributions to determination and payment of the various benefits.

Social security legislation governs many of the administrations' functions and usually sets out what is required of the institution(s) charged with running the programmes. Rules and regulations may be very detailed or may simply provide the framework of the organization, in which case the institution will regulate itself within limits which are also laid down.

B. Policy formation and direction

Given the ultimate responsibility for the overall social and economic well-being of the population, central government will certainly want to have a say in the nature of the benefits to be provided, the contents of the legislation, and the amount and allocation of funds within the framework of national economic plans.

The most frequent arrangement is for one central government department to have overall policy responsibility for social security; often this is the Ministry of Labour, or Ministry for Social Services, or for Health. There may even be a Ministry for Social Security itself. In some countries there is a Social Security Commission (or similarly named body) which is charged with policy making and oversight of social security but which still, in the final analysis, is responsible to central government. Policy making is sometimes divided between a number of central government departments and, in this case, close coordination between them is essential.

All social security insurance programmes and provident funds have one thing in common - the need to collect contributions and to account for them by properly allocating them to the personal records of participants. Means-tested and universal social security schemes, on the other hand, do not need to maintain records of employment or contributions, since the qualifying conditions for benefits are normally based on the period of residence and not on amounts of contributions and/or the length of employment.

The records for social security insurance and provident fund schemes are essential to arrive at the amount of benefit due. Qualifying periods for the long-term benefits may extend over many years and it is vital that individual records are properly maintained and easily accessible. For many years this meant that all records tended to be centralized in order to help in the identification and recording processes, particularly when workers moved from employer to employer. With the increasing use of electronic data processing (EDP) and the rapid developments in computerized systems, centralization of records is no longer of paramount importance. Whatever the system in use, each worker, employer, or other participant, must have a *unique* reference number which is retained for as long as they are associated with the social security programme.

In social insurance and provident fund schemes, employers normally deduct contributions from workers' wages or salaries. These are then paid to the relevant institution, along with the employers' contributions, as required by the regulations. Self-employed persons pay their contributions direct to the institution.

Earlier schemes used the stamp card method, stamps being purchased by the employer (or self-employed person) at the appropriate rate and then affixed to the relevant space on the individual's unique card. Relatively few schemes now use this method and, for the most part, it has been superseded by the payroll system of payment and collection of contributions. With the payroll system, employers remit contributions directly to the institution accompanied by a schedule which gives details of individual workers earnings and contributions deducted. Those details are then transferred to the participants' records, either manually or electronically.

C. Local, regional and headquarters tiers

The local level

By its very nature - responding as it does to the wide variety of individual circumstances - social security administration is a complex operation. Social security is also "very big business", for a large scheme will handle thousands of claims, make millions of benefit payments, and deal with huge sums of money during the course of a year. The organization must therefore be flexible in order to implement changes quickly. It must deal with each participant on an impartial basis.

Many social security institutions provide some form of personal service at the local level, even if claims are dealt with elsewhere in the organization. Where the institution provides offices at the local level, they are normally set up in the main population centres in order to receive claims, pay benefits and deal with questions on an individual basis. Local offices sometimes have health centres attached to them, where medical care is organized on the "direct system" (referred to in Module 3).

It is the local office which is usually responsible, in the first instance, for ensuring a satisfactory level of compliance with the law on contributions, within the local office's area. Some employers avoid their liability to pay or are frequently late in submitting the remittances in respect of contributions. The spearhead of the attack on these problems - to which even long-established schemes are not immune - is the staff at the local level. It is they who are familiar with the locality, become aware of new employers, can more easily initiate action against those who fail to comply, and are best able to enforce the law in their area.

Most schemes employ social security inspectors whose main task is to ensure a satisfactory standard of compliance. For this purpose they are usually given special powers, for example the right of entry into employers' premises and access to earnings records and related documents. It is the inspectors who routinely carry out surveys of employers and who, if all else fails, institute legal proceedings for the recovery of unpaid contributions or for other serious failures to comply with the social security law. Universal or means-tested schemes also require local representatives (inspectors) to check a person's title or continuing right to the benefit claimed, in cases of doubt.

The regional level

In many countries, especially where there are well-defined zones, provinces, or regions, the organization of the social security institution will often include a regional tier. The role of the regional office will depend on whether or not the organization has a local office tier. Where it does, the regional office will have responsibility for the oversight of local offices within the region. In this case, the regional office will not normally deal directly with the public. It will monitor the work of local offices and may also have some management functions - for example, recruitment and disposition of staff, staff training, staff welfare, etc. Local offices may also be required to submit to the regional office the unusual or more complex claims, or to obtain help with the interpretation of the law.

Where the social security institution does *not* have a local office level of administration, the regional offices will usually be directly responsible for dealing with the public - receiving claims, paying benefits, collecting contributions and undertaking compliance activities.

Headquarters - the central level

The headquarters level is responsible for the overall direction of the scheme and is particularly concerned with - for example - developing policy, responding to the requirements of the Board or Commission set up to control the scheme, research activities, the collection and interpretation of statistics, and oversight of offices at the regional level.

Where the social security programme is run by a sole government department, officers at headquarters advise the Minister in charge, often draft up new or amending legislation, frame the various instructions, are responsible for budgets, accounts and internal auditing. "Public relations", which are so essential for a proper understanding of the scheme by its participants, is usually a function for which headquarters is responsible. As mentioned earlier, in some institutions it is also the central (headquarters) level which maintains contribution accounts and records.

Clearly, the organization and range of responsibilities at the headquarters level depends on the size of the social security institution and the scope of the scheme's coverage and programme. At the one extreme, there are small schemes which have only one office which assumes *all* the functions of direction, management, evolution of policy, finance, dealing with the public, claims and payments, as well as overseeing the collection of contributions, etc. At the other extreme, there are institutions which have headquarters offices staffed by hundreds of specialists, each of whom is responsible for a specific aspect of administration.

Fig. 12:
At the one extreme ...
small offices ...
which assume all the
functions ... at the other ...
offices staffed by hundreds of
specialists ..."

UNIT 2: Other aspects of administration

A. Appeals

Every benefit claimant should have a right of appeal where benefit is refused or where there is dissatisfaction as to its quality or quantity, and this is yet another of the features of ILO Convention No. 102. The Convention does not lay down any particular avenue of appeal. In some countries the ordinary law courts are used; others set up special social security appeal bodies. Often these are tribunals consisting of a legally qualified chairman and two members drawn from lists nominated by workers' and employers' representatives respectively. Yet other countries make use of arrangements which exist under their labour legislation. Under a later Convention (No. 128 of 1967) a claimant should have the right to be represented or assisted by a qualified person of his or her own choice or, for example, by a delegate from the trade union and, although this Convention only refers to the named benefits (invalidity, old-age and survivors'), it is usual to give the same rights in all benefit cases.

Quite often a distinction is made between the interpretation of the law, on the one hand, and a point of fact, on the other. For example, it may be the case that, if benefit is claimed late, it can only be paid back to its starting date *if* there was good cause for not claiming at the right time - otherwise payment will begin from the date on which the claim was received. Whether "good cause" (for the delay) exists or not is determined on its merits and, if the social security institution refuses to pay benefit from the starting date, the claimant will have a right of appeal against that refusal. The appeal body will (after looking at the all the circumstances, evidence, etc., and possibly hearing the appellant and/or the trade union representative, and a representative from the social security office which made the decision) come to a conclusion that there was - or was not - good cause for claiming late. If the conclusion is favourable to the appellant the tribunal will then instruct that benefit be paid; if unfavourable, it will confirm the decision of the social security office.

The social security institution is also able to review a previous decision if fresh facts come to light after an unfavourable decision has been given on a claim.

Some disputes arise on highly technical matters, particularly those involving medical questions - for example, the severity of disablement following an illness or an accident at work. In such cases, it is usual to ask a medical board (consisting of two or more medically qualified personnel) to make a decision or perhaps to review a previous decision. Occasionally a special review body - for example, a medical appeal tribunal - is established to deal with cases on appeal.

There are many different ways of ensuring that the customer - the claimant - receives a fair hearing. However, in dealing with so many cases under a social security system it is inevitable that some misunderstandings will occur and it is essential that remedies for them are always available. Whether that requires the review of a decision, the processing of an appeal, or direct contact with the customer (by letter, 'phone call or interview) simply to provide an explanation, the action must be undertaken promptly.

B. The impact of computerization on administration

The computer is now commonplace in an increasing number of social security institutions. It provides the means for collecting a mass of routine information and for processing and storing it economically. The computer also enables rapid access to and retrieval of information and helps to provide the public with a more reliable and speedy service. The advent of computerized systems has also, to a great extent, helped to reduce much of the repetitive clerical work and many of the manual tasks for social security staff.

Nevertheless, there are those who view these developments with anxiety for they fear that some of the information recorded may, through human error, be incorrect and that the public may not have access to their own records in order to contest any inaccuracies in the recorded information. Increasingly, however, laws are being passed which give participants the right to know what information is stored on their records so that it can be updated and corrected where necessary. Many countries also have laws which protect this information from disclosure to third parties.

The use of computers does not, in itself, overcome basic problems stemming from poorly designed systems; it is sometimes therefore necessary to have parallel manual back-up procedures, as a safety feature, in the event of computer breakdown or loss of data.

In developing countries, it may sometimes be the case that policy dictates the use of labour-intensive procedures instead of electronic or machine processes because of the need to provide employment for a greater number of people. There may also be other problems which make investment in computerization difficult, such as the need to use hard-earned foreign currency to rent, buy and install equipment. Obtaining trained staff may also present difficulties and those who obtain training are often subsequently tempted to move into the private sector where very often pay is higher.

Some of these problems can be overcome by sharing facilities with other users (for example, other government departments) but, if this solution is used, caution is needed to ensure that computer time *is* available when needed and that there is adequate protection of the confidentiality of claimants' records.

C. *Migrant workers*

During their working lives, people may move from job to job, perhaps in the same village or town or from one region to another, in search of work or better-paid prospects. A nationwide social security programme should be able to ensure that, when the time comes for them to claim benefit, records of all their employment(s), of all contributions paid, and residence details, are quickly brought to hand and are easily accessible.

There are, however, some groups of workers whose jobs take them to other countries and away from the immediate protection of their own national social security system. These might include, for example, seafarers, international airline personnel, persons serving their country abroad as diplomats or consular officials, construction workers, and sales representatives who go abroad on foreign contracts.

Over the years, many social security insurance programmes have been extended in order to maintain special coverage for such groups, for example by arranging for the continuation of compulsory cover for limited periods (e.g. 12 months) so as to bridge the gap which might otherwise open up in their social security records.

In the past, however, once people moved to another country - whether or not they took up employment there - they lost the social security cover which they had previously enjoyed in their "home" country. Although they could perhaps have then come within the cover of a social security programme in the "new" country, they sometimes found themselves up against restrictive rules. Such restrictions may have covered nationality and residence conditions, the need to serve new qualifying periods of employment or contributions, the absence of cover for dependants, etc.. This was clearly unjust, the more so since many migrant workers were vulnerable and less able to clearly make their arguments for continued protection to their "home" authority or to that of the "new" country.

A number of well-established social security systems tried to overcome at least some of those difficulties by making what are referred to as "reciprocal agreements" with neighbouring countries to which their nationals traditionally migrated. By the end of the 1950s, in Europe and even further afield, a network of these bilateral agreements had been established.

The ILO had done - and continues to do - much to encourage these international agreements. As early as 1919, when adopting the Unemployment Convention (No. 2) at its very first Session, the International Labour Conference directed that member States, bound by the Convention, who had established an unemployment insurance scheme should make arrangements which would permit workers of one State, but working in the territory of another, to receive benefits equal to those paid to workers who were nationals of the second State. Many Conventions have been adopted since then, all designed to encourage equality of treatment in social security, no matter what the worker's nationality and regardless of where they were working.

Basic principles

The actual terms of social security agreements between any two countries are bound to vary widely, and the contents of national legislation differ greatly; nevertheless, five basic principles for their application can be identified. (It is not intended to do more than outline these principles in this publication, as a more comprehensive explanation is given in Chapter 15 of the ILO publication *INTRODUCTION TO SOCIAL SECURITY**).

The five principles relate to:

- Equality of treatment - the immigrant worker should have, as far as possible, the same rights and obligations under the law and should receive benefits on the same terms as national workers in the country of immigration.

- The determination of the applicable legislation - the migrant worker should know clearly which law specifically covers him/ her.

- The maintenance of the migrant worker's acquired rights - any right to benefits which s/he has acquired (or any prospective right) should be guaranteed, even if it has been acquired in the other territory.

*INTRODUCTION TO SOCIAL SECURITY -International Labour Office, Geneva. ISBN 92-2-103638-3)

- The maintenance of rights which are being acquired - so that if benefit title is dependent on the completion of a particular qualifying period, account should be taken of periods served by the migrant worker in all the countries which are a party to the agreement.

- The absence of restrictions on the payment of benefits abroad - an increasingly important feature in international relations in the social security field.

The mechanism for dealing with benefit claims arising out of the increasing international mobility of labour is quite complex. After the conclusion of an agreement of a bilateral or multilateral nature between countries, administrative arrangements are usually drawn up between officials of the institutions concerned and claims are often handled by special departments within the appropriate social security institutions. Benefit may derive from one law only, or from two or more of the national laws involved, in proportion to the periods during which the worker was covered under the law. It may be that the claimant will have partial entitlement under *each* national law, or a single entitlement, with some form of financial adjustment being made between the countries involved.

It is important to remember that whatever the techniques they all have the same objective - to give migrant workers and their families complete social security protection which might otherwise be denied to them.

Extension of scope

The five principles referred to above have increasingly been extended to operate for non-contributory (as well as contributory) benefits - i.e. in respect of those benefits which are largely or entirely financed from public funds. This is a more recent trend which recognizes that the effective participation of migrant workers, in the financing of national social security programmes, is not limited to social security contributions which may be deducted from wages; migrant workers also make a contribution through the work they perform and/or by paying taxes to the public funds of the country in which they are presently working.

Finally, it should be noted that the ILO itself has taken the initiative to supplement its own Conventions (concerned as they are with a statement of fundamental principles and the definition of general methods of coordination) by helping to evolve regional and subregional instruments aimed at bringing groups of countries more closely together in the social security field. It has devised model articles which lay down the principles for countries to follow, together with draft administrative arrangements which countries may use - in whole or in part - to operate any agreements that are entered into. The ILO has also been closely involved with a considerable number of multilateral agreements which are of great importance, some examples of which are those for the Central Commission for Rhine Navigation, the Council of Europe, the European Communities, the Organization of Central American States, the Common African and Mauritian Organization, and the Andean Group of Countries.

As explained in the introduction to this Module, only a very brief reference has been made to social security administration as a much more comprehensive examination is undertaken in the Manual entitled *ADMINISTRATION OF SOCIAL SECURITY* (Manual number 2 in the series) which includes detailed reference to:

- Coverage and registration.

- Collecting and recording contributions (including computerized systems).

- Compliance and enforcement.

- Award and payment of benefit.

- Public relations.

- Management of social security institutions

    - Managing human resources
    - Monitoring performance

SOCIAL SECURITY PRINCIPLES

MODULE 6:
THE ROLE OF THE INTERNATIONAL LABOUR ORGANIZATION IN SOCIAL SECURITY

International Labour Office - Geneva

MODULE CONTENTS

MODULE 6

THE ROLE OF THE INTERNATIONAL LABOUR ORGANIZATION IN SOCIAL SECURITY

UNIT 1: International labour standards

Many references have been made throughout the Manual to the International Labour Organization - the ILO - and, in particular, to the Conventions and Recommendations adopted in the field of social security by the International Labour Conference. It will have been apparent, throughout the Manual, that the ILO has played an important role in relation to social security development.

The prime concern of the ILO is the formulation of international policies and programmes to improve working and living conditions. One of the principal ways in which it does so is through international labour *Conventions*, the drafting of which involves the ILO secretariat in extensive study and discussion, and in the examination of existing laws and practices throughout the world.

Convention
A *Convention* is a set of firm criteria for the preparation of national legislation and, when it has been adopted by the annual International Labour Conference, member States of the ILO are required by the Constitution to bring the Convention to the notice of their legislative authorities. In due course, if the standards which have been set are embodied in national laws, the States concerned will be in a position to ratify the Convention. Not every State which follows the Convention necessarily proceeds to ratification, but the influence of the ILO in setting standards is effective regardless of the formal procedures involved.

Recommendations
Recommendations are international instruments, similar to Conventions, but not subject to the formal process of ratification. A *Recommendation* lays down detailed standards

which it is desirable should be achieved, often on subjects for which a Convention was considered too rigid a procedure. Where a Convention is accompanied by a Recommendation, the latter will suggest certain lines of advance beyond the limits defined in the more mandatory Articles of the Convention.

Fig. 13:
"... ILO ... formulation of ...policies and programmes ... throught ... Conventions ... and Recommendations ..."

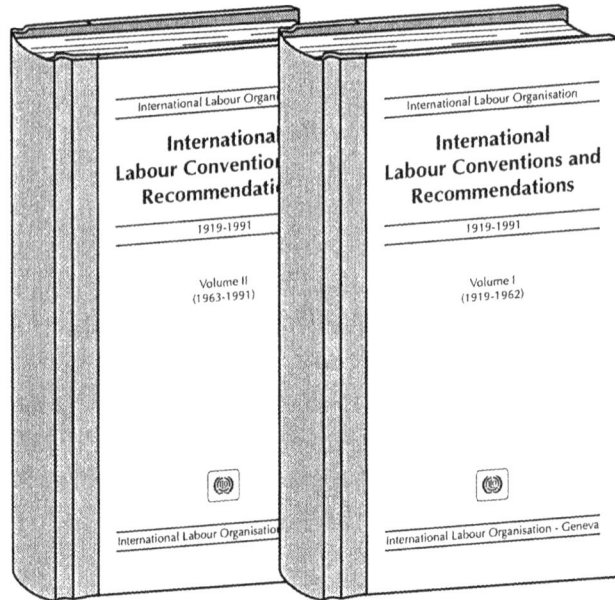

It is not too bold to say that ILO Conventions and Recommendations have had a marked influence on the shaping of social security programmes throughout the world, in setting norms and standards, and by giving guidance.

The ILO was established by the peace settlement of 1919 and has a Constitution which requires it to bring together, at an annual conference, tripartite delegations of its member States - that is to say workers, employers and governments. The wording of the Constitution includes reference to "the protection of the worker against sickness, disease and injury arising out of employment, provision for old age and injury, protection of the interests of workers when employed in countries other than their own ...."

The ILO is one of the senior of the specialized agencies which originally formed part of the League of Nations and it is now one of the members of the family of the United Nations. It has its Headquarters (the International Labour Office) at Geneva, Switzerland, and has regional and area offices throughout the world. The International Labour Conference elects a Governing Body, which is also tripartite in nature, and the Governing Body elects the Director-General of the International Labour Office.

Among the many departments at ILO Headquarters is one (referred to as SEC SOC) which is concerned exclusively with social security. In addition, there are a number of social security advisers, at several locations throughout the world, who are attached to multi-disciplinary teams of ILO specialists or to ILO Regional Offices.

Reference was made, in an earlier section, to the fact that relatively few member States had anything approaching a comprehensive social security programme when the ILO was established in 1919. Such programmes as did exist at that time were mostly insurance-based, with "workmen's compensation" employer liability schemes predominating - although a number of countries had "poor law" provisions to fall back on for individuals who were destitute. By 1995, however, 165 countries had a formal social security programme. During and immediately after the Second World War the ILO broadened its view of social security (which, until that time, had tended to concentrate on social insurance programmes) and turned its attention to *all* types of social protection programmes - those which have been discussed in this manual.

This new departure was marked by the adoption of a landmark Recommendation - the Income Security Recommendation, 1944 (No. 67). It was accompanied by a Recommendation specifically relating to health care - the Medical Care Recommendation, 1944 (No. 69) - which proposed, among other things, that all members of a community should have access to health services on the basis of universality.

A further landmark in international social security was the adoption, in 1952, of the Social Security (Minimum Standards) Convention (No.102) - already referred to many times throughout this manual - which brought together, in one comprehensive document, the policies to which the then member States were prepared to subscribe, and defined the range of benefits which form the core of social security. It laid down minimum requirements as to coverage of the population and the content and level of benefits, and covered the protection of the rights of contributors and beneficiaries, and ancillary matters of administration.

Convention No.102 maintains its authority as setting important basic standards even though, in the meantime, the ILO has moved on to a series of more detailed Conventions on specific branches of social security.

These are listed at the end of this section, together with a number of Recommendations, for ease of reference. ILO Convention (No.102) brought together many elements which had been incorporated in earlier, separate, instruments. It attempted to be comprehensive, covering the full nine contingencies for benefit and seeking to extend coverage to the whole population. While a State may ratify the whole Convention if in a position to do so, flexibility of application was achieved by allowing a State to accept *parts* of the Convention, according to its own needs and stage of development. Furthermore - and this was a novel feature - a developing country "whose economy and medical facilities are insufficiently developed" was able to claim exemption from some of the more exacting standards - and even from the minimum standards.

As already seen, there have been further social security Conventions which have, in general, set higher standards in such aspects as the coverage of the population and/or the level of benefits. However, Convention No. 102 remains very much in force, embodying the basic minimum targets for each branch of benefit and setting out the broad framework of common standards to encourage the widest development of social security programmes.

Thus, over the years, a comprehensive set of principles has evolved but how are they translated into action? The methods vary and include the setting of standards (the targets to be achieved) which can only be arrived at following study and research, practical technical assistance by field staff, coupled with a programme of training, in cooperation with national and international bodies.

Social Security Conventions and Recommendations

Conventions

No. 102   Social Security (Minimum Standards) 1952

No. 103   Maternity Protection (Revised) 1952

No. 118   Equality of Treatment (Social Security) 1962

No. 121   Employment Injury Benefits 1964

No. 128   Invalidity, Old-age, Survivors' Benefits 1967

No. 130   Medical Care and Sickness Benefits 1969

No. 157   Maintenance of Social Security rights 1982

No. 165   Social Security (Seafarers) (Revised) 1987

No. 168   Employment Promotion and Protection against Unemployment 1988

Recommendations

No. 95   Maternity Protection 1952

No. 121   Employment Injury Benefits 1964

No. 131   Invalidity, Old-age and Survivors' Benefits 1967

No. 134   Medical care and Sickness Benefits 1969

No. 162   Older Workers 1980

No. 167   Maintenance of Social Security Rights 1983

No. 176   Employment Promotion and Protection against Unemployment 1988

UNIT 2: Other functions of the ILO

A. *Studies and research*

To undertake the work required of it by its member States, the ILO must keep abreast of current trends. If it is to give competent advice about adaptations of programmes, or the establishment of new schemes, the ILO's Social Security Department must acquire the knowledge and experience to be able to do so.

Research activities which are carried out are three-pronged. Firstly, there is work connected with policies and standards; secondly, particular subjects of concern are studied in depth; and, thirdly, training material and information must be made available to those who require it.

On the first activity - policies and standards - a vast amount of time-consuming research work is carried out, for it is necessary to establish the up-to-date position with regard to the laws and practices of social security throughout the world. This material is used not only for possible consideration of Conventions or Recommendations but for regional and other conferences, as well as by countries wishing to change or develop their social protection programmes. Between 1919 and 1989 some of the more important national social security laws and subordinate legislation were published in three languages in the ILO's Legislative Series (replaced by Labour Law Documents from 1989).

The second major activity - in-depth studies - requires that the Social Security Department looks at social security related matters which are of concern in today's world, as well as those which are likely to affect social security programmes in the future. The many publications which have appeared over the years bear witness to the range of studies which are either prepared by the research staff of the Department or specially commissioned from external consultants and experts. One regular major periodical publication is *The Cost of Social Security*, which contains data relating to the financial operations of an increasing number of social security schemes, in both industrialized and developing countries, and which attempts to provide an international comparison of these data. Another of the ILO's publications - the bi-monthly International Labour Review - frequently contains articles on major social security aspects.

The third major activity of the Department relates to training and the dissemination of information. Training publications are produced for administrative officials of social security programmes, some of which have a deliberate regional bias or treat specialized subjects in a detailed way. The ILO has an important body of documentation on a broad range of social security topics and issues. Items are available, on request, to those who need information and reports.

B. Technical cooperation

The ILO has given practical assistance and advice to member States for many years. In the early days this usually meant short exploratory or advisory missions from the Geneva headquarters and, despite the growth of and the accumulating expertise in social security round the world, there is still no shortage of requests for help.

Three principal methods of undertaking technical assistance work are used by the ILO. The first is to assign ILO staff members, and/or external experts or consultants, to the country concerned; the second, to provide fellowships for training; and, lastly, training courses may be organized.

Missions to countries by ILO staff, external experts or consultants, are undertaken for a variety of reasons. Examples include: pre-planning broad or limited social security programmes; helping with the drafting of legislation; setting up the administration of a scheme; improving the administrative capability of existing programmes; providing advice or direct help in the design and installation of computerized systems. Financial and actuarial advice is also a very important feature of ILO technical assistance projects.

Work on technical cooperation projects is often very demanding for, apart from the technical qualifications required, it calls for tact and diplomacy, an ability to adapt quickly to the different conditions, cultures and attitudes which prevail in the host countries, and to take all these into account when giving help and offering advice.

A most important part of any mission is an early contact with the appropriate representatives of workers, employers and government. Given the tripartite structure of the ILO, these contacts are vital and go far beyond the simple need for courtesy. Such contacts are of considerable help to experts and consultants and quickly provide invaluable insights into local attitudes, needs and circumstances.

Fig. 14:
*"... contact with appropriate
... representatives ... workers,
employers and Government"*

Fellowship programmes enable social security officials from developing countries to receive training in other social security institutions. Normally this entails a period of attachment to one or more social security organizations outside the person's home country.

ILO officials regularly participate in social security training courses, seminars and meetings, including those organized by the International Social Security Association (ISSA). When working "in the field" - on country projects - it is common for ILO consultants and experts to be invited to address meetings of workers' organizations and employers' associations and they frequently participate in training courses run by trade unions and by workers' education groups.

It is appropriate, in this section on technical cooperation, to include a reference to the financing of ILO technical assistance projects. Some are financed by the ILO itself, through its regular budget programme, but normally these are projects of only a short duration. Other agencies, for example the United Nations Development Programme (UNDP), also make arrangements for technical cooperation to be carried out and, on occasions, the UNDP will ask the ILO to execute projects, particularly when the project has a social security content.

Other organizations, such as the World Bank or the development banks, will plan a project along with the ILO and the government concerned, and then ask the ILO to execute the project. Several industrialized countries collaborate directly with the United Nations and its specialised agencies - including the ILO - to provide technical assistance, and there are also countries which are prepared to meet the whole or part of the cost of a project, through a bilateral agreement, but which then ask the ILO to provide the technical input.

C. International cooperation

The Social Security Department of the ILO maintains close relationships with a large number of bodies which are active in the field of social protection. Of particular importance is the working relationship with the International Social Security Association (ISSA) which was founded in 1927 under the auspices of the ILO.

While the ILO *serves* member States, the ISSA is a grouping of "... services, institutions or bodies administering one or more branches of social security or mutual benefit schemes". ISSA operates on a worldwide basis and every three years it holds a General Assembly. Permanent technical committees deal with an array of topics - medical care and sickness insurance; insurance against employment injury and occupational disease; unemployment insurance and employment maintenance; old-age, invalidity and survivors' insurance; family benefit; the prevention of occupational risks; organization and methods; and common subjects, such as legal, actuarial and statistical questions.

The ISSA holds technical and research meetings, and regional training courses. It also supplies members with periodical publications including the International Social Security Review, and has built up a central reference library of many thousands of social security publications from all over the world.

Among the other bodies which should be mentioned are the Inter-American Committee on Social Security, to which the ILO has provided technical and financial support in the Committee's efforts to develop, reform and improve social security in the American region; close contacts are maintained with the Organization of American States, the Pan American Health Organization and the Ibero-American Social Security Organization.

In Africa, contacts continue with the Organization of African Unity to develop suitable training courses in social security - not only for staff members of the social security institutions but also for the workers' and employers' representatives who participate in the formulation and direction of policy through their membership of statutory boards and advisory committees. Contacts have also been established with a number of sub-regional organizations in Africa, to deal, amongst others, with the question of protection of migrant workers' rights.

FURTHER READING

Pierre Mouton:
Social security in Africa: Trends, problems and prospects
(Geneva, 1976).

Social security for the unemployed (Geneva, 1976).

Social security for migrant workers (Geneva, 1977).

Social security for teachers (Geneva, 1979).

The ILO/Norway African regional training course for senior social security managers and administrative officials
(Geneva, 1983).

Maintenance of rights in social security, Report V, International Labour Conference, 69th Session (Geneva, 1983).

Financing social security: The options
(Geneva, 1984).

Into the twenty-first century. The development of social security (Geneva, 1984).

Introduction to social security (Geneva, 3rd ed., 1984).

World Labour Report 1, Ch. 6, "Social security in the highly industrialized countries", pp. 151-173 (Geneva, 1984).

World Labour Report 3, Ch. 2, sec. 3, "Social insurance and social assistance", pp. 38-43 (Geneva, 1987).

From pyramid to pillar. Population change and social security in Europe (Geneva, 1989).

World Labour Report 4, Ch. 4, sec. 2, "Public-private comparison of social security protection", pp. 96-103
(Geneva, 1989).

A.-M. Brocas, A.-M. Cailloux and V. Oger: **Women and social security: Progress towards equality of treatment**
(Geneva, 1990).

A. Ron et al.: **Health insurance in developing countries**
(Geneva, 1990).

The ILO and the elderly (Geneva, 1992).

World Labour Report 5, Ch. 4, sec. "Social protection in Eastern Europe and the former Soviet Union", pp. 69-74 (Geneva, 1992).

World Labour Report 6, Ch. 4, "Social protection and economic adjustment in developing countries", pp. 53-64 (Geneva, 1993).

World Labour Report 7, Ch.3, "Health care in developing countries", pp. 67-77 (Geneva 1994)

World Labour Report 8, Ch.2, "Ageing societies: Problems and prospects for older workers", pp. 31-54. Ch.3, "Privatization, employment and social protection", pp. 55-67. (Geneva 1995)

The cost of social security (1987-1989);
(Geneva, 1996) ISBN 92-2-007348-X; ISSN 0538-8295

Social Security Programs Throughout the World - 1995. Social Security Administration, Office of Research and Statistics. SSA Publication number 13-11805. July 1995. Research Report #64. ISBN 0-16-048224-0

Employing foreign workers, ***A manual on policies and procedures of special interest to middle- and low-income.*** ISBN 92-2-109453-7. (Geneva 1996)

Sending workers abroad, ***A manual of low- and middle-income countries.*** ISBN 92-2-108525-2. (Geneva 1997).

www.ingramcontent.com/pod-product-compliance
Lightning Source LLC
Chambersburg PA
CBHW080841270326
41927CB00013B/3061